Selected poems
Rogha dánta

Selected poems
Rogha dánta

SEÁN Ó RÍORDÁIN

IN EAGAR AG / EDITED BY

FRANK SEWELL

YALE UNIVERSITY PRESS ■ NEW HAVEN & LONDON

IN ASSOCIATION WITH CLÓ IAR-CHONNACHT ■ INDREABHÁN

A MARGELLOS
WORLD REPUBLIC OF LETTERS BOOK

The Margellos World Republic of Letters is dedicated to making literary works from around the globe available in English through translation. It brings to the English-speaking world the work of leading poets, novelists, essayists, philosophers, and playwrights from Europe, Latin America, Africa, Asia, and the Middle East to stimulate international discourse and creative exchange.

Copyright © 2014 by Yale University and Cló Iar-Chonnacht.

Yale University Press books may be purchased in quantity for educational, business, or promotional use. For information, please e-mail sales.press@yale.edu (U.S. office) or sales@yaleup.co.uk (U.K. office).

Set in Electra and Nobel types by Keystone Typesetting, Inc.
Printed in the United States of America.

The Library of Congress has cataloged the hardcover edition as follows:

Ó Ríordáin, Sean, 1916–1977.
[Poems. Selections]
Selected poems / Sean Ó Ríordáin ; edited by Frank Sewell.
     p. cm. — (Margellos world republic of letters)
Includes bibliographical references.
ISBN 978-0-300-19058-8 (cloth : alk. paper)
I. Sewell, Frank, 1968–. II. Title.
PB1399.O72A6 2013
891.6′214 — dc23
2012037880

ISBN 978-0-300-24018-4 (pbk.)

A catalogue record for this book is available from the British Library.

This paper meets the requirements of ANSI/NISO Z39.48-1992 (Permanence of Paper).
10 9 8 7 6 5 4 3 2 1

for Bob Welch (1947–2013)

CONTENTS

FROM *BROSNA* (1964)

FROM *LÍNTE LIOMBÓ* (1971)

FROM *TAR ÉIS MO BHÁIS* (1978)

FOREWORD

FREEDOM

I'm going down among the ordinary people.
I'm going to get up on my own two feet and go right
down to where they're gathered tonight.
I'm going down in search of some good old Servitude
instead of this poisonous Freedom stuff
that turns out to be so grim and gruff.
I'll try to restrain the pack of thoughts
snarling and snapping at my heels
through the great loneliness I tend to feel.
I'll go looking for a holy chapel
with a huge crowd that'll have gathered in it
at a time nailed down to the nearest minute.
I'll go looking for the company of those
who could never see
the point of being cut off and free.
I'll listen to the two cents worth
they'll rearrange
like so much spare change.
I'll try to show a little respect to the people
who still can't stand
any idea that isn't second-hand.

I'll stick with you day and night,
keeping my head down,
staying loyal only to the crop-crown.
I've had thoughts springing of late in my skull,
these thoughts springing of late
unruly and intemperate.
But I'll try to give my attention
to things that are all tied up,
to every dogged idea and its pup, yup.
To power, to contracts drawn up by the hour, to ex cathedra
pronouncements, to the predictable word,
to the hours riding herd.
To the vice-abbot, the clock-face, the timeserving servant,
to the comparison that falls apart,
to the chicken-heart.
To the mousy one, the measured one, the flea-sized flea,
to quoting chapter and verse,
to the cursive alphabet that's more a curse.
To all those majestic to-ings and fro-ings,
to the nightly casting of dice,
to the once-blessed, the thrice-.
To the farmer riddling the autumn wind
as he looks out over a field
of barley and contemplates its yield.
To partnering in insight, partnering in memory,
to buying into a start-up when we could have stopped it,
to the co-opting of the co-opted.
For I'm here to rail now and forever

against Freedom and all its works,
against everything about independence that irks.
The mind that falls into the deep furrow of Freedom
will never spring up afresh.
That mind is pre-trampled. Pre-threshed.
There aren't any God-made hills in that vicinity
but abstract hills, hills of the imagination
keeping their own hard station.
Every last one of these hills is coming down
with wishes and deep desires
that never meet the goals to which they aspire.
There are no limits to the idea of Freedom
nor the range of the imagination. There are no bounds
to any of those deep desires. There's no reprieve to be found.

trans. Paul Muldoon *

*Ó Ríordáin's original poem 'Saoirse' and his own translation are included
later in this selection.

EDITOR'S PREFACE

'Travels from self to self': The poetry of Seán Ó Ríordáin[1]

Part One

Seán Ó Ríordáin (1916–77) published three collections of his own original poetry during his lifetime: *Eireaball Spideoige* (1952), *Brosna* (1964) and *Línte Liombó* (1971). Ó Ríordáin also co-translated into modern Irish a selection of devotional lyrics written between the ninth and twelfth centuries: *Rí na nUile* (1967). This comparatively small output is due partly to the vast scale of his first collection *Eireaball Spideoige* (1952) which featured no fewer than fifty-three poems. The rest of the poet's life was dogged periodically with illness, self-doubt, and also journalistic commitments, which combined to reduce his creative output. His final volume, *Tar Éis Mo Bháis* (1978), was published posthumously.

This does not seem to be a prolific amount of work, in comparison with poets such as Máirtín Ó Direáin (1910–88) or, for example, Eavan Boland or Cathal Ó Searcaigh today. But there is no doubt that the quality of his output makes Ó Ríordáin a central figure not only in twentieth-century Irish-language poetry but in twentieth-century Irish poetry as a whole. His presence is acknowledged in the inclusion of his poems in major anthologies of Irish poetry;[2] in poems (not all of them in Irish) addressed to him[3] or about him;[4] in the thoughts that he set dancing in the heads of other poets who felt the need to respond, or position themselves in relation, to him;[5] in the work of poets for whom Ó Ríordáin has become a 'second conscience';[6] in the ever-growing list of critical analyses of his oeuvre;[7] in the many translations of his poems that have appeared during and after his lifetime;[8] and in the continuing demand of the public to read more of his writing in general—from his journalism to his diaries. In fact, since the publication of Seán Ó Coileáin's revealing biography in 1982, interest among readers and critics in Ó Ríordáin's contribution to Irish literature and cultural thought has steadily increased.

For the most part, however, knowledge and appreciation of this poet's work has naturally enough been mostly a privilege enjoyed by Irish-language readers and scholars. Ó Ríordáin may have had doubts including about himself as a writer and even (at times) his very hold upon the language, but Irish was the language in which poems 'happened'[9] for him while, in his terms, he was 'present'[10] or awake enough to receive them. Likewise, the linguistic 'excitement' or frisson that sparked poetry for him occurred in Irish.[11] Reading his diaries, one clearly sees that, as Cathal Ó Searcaigh has said of himself, Irish was the language of his emotions; the language in which, and with which, he found his own truly original and creative voice. That voice is well known in the Irish-language community. So why produce a 'selected poems' and, more controversially perhaps, a *bilingual* selected poems now?

One reason is to reappraise Ó Ríordáin as a poet. This seems necessary since the repeated selection of particular poems for translation in various anthologies increasingly provides an unremittingly dark impression of the poet as someone concerned almost exclusively with religion, illness and death or, even worse, as a writer trapped in the Joycean nets of language, nationality and religion. The greater space afforded in this text (compared to a necessarily small section in an anthology) will hopefully show that Ó Ríordáin's work is somewhat wider in range and tone than any such characterisation would suggest; and that even when he does tackle such delicate and potentially debilitating subjects as Joyce identified, he manages (like Joyce) to fly into, out of and around them. In doing so, moreover, he produces striking images and haunting phrases in poems that not only struggle with, but actually explore those 'nets,' freshly questioning and examining them along with other recurrent concerns.

A second reason for producing this bilingual selection is simply to honour Ó Ríordáin as a poet who himself was in the habit of reading literature both *in* other languages (including Latin) and in translation *from* many other languages (including Russian and French). It seems only fair and highly deserved, in fact, that the 'riversound' of his work should join the ocean of international literature in translation—not for his own original poems to be 'drowned' like the poet-speaker in 'Cnoc Mellerí'/'Mount Melleray,' but for them to *sound* out in Irish and be broadcast[12] here in *two* languages (and even more in future[13]) to a larger audience or 'crowd' than he ruefully envisaged in 'Éisteacht chúng'/'Minority audience' (*Brosna*, p. 38).

A favourite word of Ó Ríordáin's was 'blas'/a taste or flavour, and it is sincerely hoped that the 'taste' of his work provided in this selection will entice readers to read his entire poetic oeuvre—edited by Seán Ó Coileáin and published by Cló Iar-Chonnacht in 2011. There is simply no substitute for reading Ó Ríordáin's poems in the language of their composition. But for readers without Irish, it would be a pity if they were also entirely without Ó Ríordáin, and missed out, for example, on his satiric humour and much-neglected love poetry. Given his original poems contained in this selection, readers will be very much *with* the poet; and given the translations, they will be with him for as long a time and as full an extent as is realistically possible through the medium of a second language, despite the over-rehearsed difficulties of translating poetry in particular.

Yet, even if all that English-language readers of this text get from the translations is just a 'taste' of Ó Ríordáin's work, that taste will be worthwhile. It will certainly be better than the nothing which one English-language daughter and heir seemed to know about Máire Mhac an tSaoi when the latter was writing at the height of her powers: 'If I had looked closely . . . I might have noticed that there were no women poets, old or young, past or present in my immediate environment.'[14] Thankfully, Ó Ríordáin, at least, has been well and truly 'noticed' by readers and by subsequent generations of poets, with lines from his oeuvre, for example, forming epigraphs or starting points in poems by members of the *INNTI* generation, including Cathal Ó Searcaigh and Michael Davitt.[15] Ó Ríordáin's voice, as Alan Titley has pointed out,[16] continues to echo in the skull of his readers, among them leading writers of the next two generations of poets in Irish after him, including Nuala Ní Dhomhnaill and Gearóid Mac Lochlainn.[17]

Less visibly, Ó Ríordáin has also made a lasting impression on many English-language writers in Ireland. Some of them along with their comrades-in-Irish[18] (Ó Ríordáin's direct heirs) contribute translations to the current volume, willingly giving of their time, talent and energy in response to particular poems with enough of a *beo-gheit*/living jumpstart in them to overcome linguistic partition. Translation, to paraphrase Dylan Thomas, is more a 'craft' than a 'sullen art,' so there is necessarily much craftiness at work in any translation of a poem, and certainly of an Ó Ríordáin poem. Anything less, such as the fool's gold of word-for-word literalism, would turn a lyric in one language into a random list of lines in another; would be, as Ó Ríordáin once put it (in a recurring whirlpool of doubt about his own aesthetics, audience and medium), to 'unwrite' poems into 'un-poetry.'[19] Instead, like all world literature worthy of the name, Ó Ríordáin's work deserves to be read and re-read, interpreted and re-interpreted, translated and re-translated by each new generation.

Part Two

Seán Ó Ríordáin began writing, and continued to fuel his writing, by noting down his observations and ideas in a diary from 1935 on. His surviving notes were first recorded in a 'leabhar cuntais'/an account book dating back to 1940.[20] Literally and symbolically, this provided him with a space in which he could bring himself, his life, times, meetings and musings to account. In addition it was also very much a *writer's* journal which allowed him free (and private) rein to play with words, to 'riff' on phrases, ideas and alliterations. Many of these would later be further distilled or 'sifted' ('scagtha') until they ended up forming part of a poem or one of his regular *Irish Times* articles (1967–75). The account book also allowed him to work through and word his responses to his reading which was impressively wide in terms of genre and region, including, for example, Russian masters of the short story such as Turgenev and Chekhov; Scandinavian dramatists such as Ibsen and Strindberg; Rabelaisian novelists such as Cervantes and Rabelais himself; American poets as wide and varied as Emily Dickinson, e e cummings and T. S. Eliot; also the bard of Avon, Marcus Aurelius and sundry linguists and philosophers from Raïssa Maritain to St Augustine, not to mention the full historical canon of Irish literature (in both of its main languages) from early to modern times.[21]

Ó Ríordáin's habit of recording thoughts and impressions, of doodling in prose (and sometimes even in pictures[22]) increasingly became something that he felt compelled to do; it served part of his nature, that of a genuine artist and inquisitive intellectual of his time. Without it, he said on more than one occasion, he would have been lost;[23] and worse, for us, much of his work would have been lost or never written. Instead it would have joined his other unrecorded thoughts that slipped away into oblivion, as noted in poems such as 'Sa séipéal dom'/'In the chapel' (*LL* p. 18) or here in 'Roithleán'/ 'Whirl.' Thankfully this poet was not content to leave the stage of this world with an 'aigne neamhscríte'/'an unrecorded mind' ('Tost'/'Silence'). Instead, he opened himself to 'fuaim na habhann'/the 'riversound,' to the low-key ambience of 'Cláirseach shean na ngnáthrud'/ 'The venerable harp of the mundane,' to the word-'music' or 'Ceol' of literature in other languages from Welsh to Latin, and to the playful possibilities of his medium, the Irish language itself, in poems such as 'Scagadh'/Sifting (*ES* p. 110) and 'Siollabadh'/'Syllabled' or syllabl-ing. This range and inventiveness, his ability to hit true notes that still last and resonate for Irish speakers and writers today[24] is born, however, of an almost unbearable tension. On the one hand, Ó Ríordáin was sustained by tradition, by the old Gaelic poets whom he called upon in 'A sheanfhilí, múinídh dom glao'/'Old poets, teach me the call,' and by more recent guardians such as Daniel Corkery (celebrated here in 'Do Dhomhnall Ó Corcora'); but on the other hand, he felt the tug of his own ego, his own 'cead cainte'[25]/permission to speak for himself, his own 'Saoirse' or 'Liberty.' He was painfully torn, therefore, between Corkery and Joycery, between strict adherence to a straight-line (phallic?) concept of tradition and the tangential, zig-zagging trajectory once noted and advocated by Ralph Waldo Emerson[26] and more recently, and more locally, by Seamus Heaney.[27] Caught between these magnetic poles and leaning at various times more towards Corkery than to Joycery, before changing position again, Ó Ríordáin well knew that he was living out the tension between the not-so-much 'either/or' but 'both/and' of (what T. S. Eliot termed) 'tradition *and* the individual talent.' This meant that Ó Ríordáin was playing on no 'dead slack string' (as poet Patrick Kavanagh once thought was possible[28]) but on his own nerves, often stretched beyond breaking point.[29] See, for example, 'Na fathaigh'/'The giants.'

Part Three

Ó Ríordáin's poetry has seven main themes:

1. writing or poetry itself and its place in his life;
2. the plural self (sometimes versus the longing for a single, integral self);
3. the relationship between the independent individual or art-

ist and the 'people' (including a very much dual attitude to-
wards this relationship);

4. gender and even genetic relations, linked concerns that
   were complicated for the poet by his inheritance of TB and
   his consequent isolation, and by sexist notions then promul-
   gated by the Catholic Church which divided (as he put it)
   'an mhaidin álainn/'na fireann is 'na baineann' ('the beau-
   tiful morning/into male and female'), and which would put
   'coir drúise in intinn na n-éan' ('the sin of lust into the
   mind of birds'), filling the world 'with shame';[30]
5. the nature and condition of animals, including sometimes a
   comparison between people and animals, and what this
   might suggest about the nature of the human;
6. the Irish language itself and what it is like to be writing in
   the mid-twentieth century in a minority and/but national
   language, a concern reflecting his own increasing engage-
   ment with Irish as a medium and, latterly, as a subject fol-
   lowing strict linguistic criticism of some of his early work;
7. and, finally, that gentleman caller, 'Mister Death,' an entity
   that Ó Ríordáin unsurprisingly had a lot to say about, given
   that TB left him in imminent anticipation of death for most
   of his life, physically struggling for breath as evidenced in
   his speech and, arguably, in the shorter and shorter lines
   and poems of his later work where each comma or line-
   ending marks not just a thought-or image-space but a much
   needed breath-space, too.

Some of his poems span two themes or categories at the same time:
'Préachán'/'Crow,' for example, could be (superficially) categorized
as an animal poem but more importantly reflects upon gender and
sexuality in changing times. This one example, however, serves to
highlight the diverse, and sometimes inter-related, nature of Ó Ríor-

dáin's concerns, together with his varied treatment, over time, of them.

Studying his poems from today's vantage point, it is striking that he seems to have repeatedly tuned in to a *zeitgeist* or, rather, to have worked his own way towards concepts and aesthetics which he did not always read about directly from others but which he came to share or express in his own way. It is as if, as an artist, he arrived (through artistic practice) at conclusions that the 'theory-vendors' (Kavanagh's term for literary critics) philosophised towards: for example, to read Ó Ríordáin's introduction to *Eireaball Spideoige* or his diaries which insist that the creation of art or poetry demands the 'open' mind or fresh-eyed vision of a child together with 'immersion' or total concentration on the external object or scene in order to convey it, is to be reminded of Viktor Shklosky's Russian Formalist concept of '*ostranenie*/defamiliarization.'[31]

Similarly, it is remarkable to re-read Ó Ríordáin's many poems which fret over, or finally accept, the incorrigible plurality of the self, especially those gathered in his 1978 collection (*Tar Éis Mo Bháis*, published just one year after his death), when one realises that while he was working on those poems, William Coles was working on his own famous 1978 text, *The Plural I.*[33] Ó Ríordáin's ruminations on this topic range from 'Oileán agus oileán eile'/'This island and the other island' in which an essential, authentic self is held in reverence, to fear of its loss in 'Línte Liombó'/'Limbo lines,' and gallows humour at the unavoidable shedding of skins or selves in 'Rian na gcos'/'The footprints.' The semi-mournful, semi-comic acceptance of cast-off selves or layers in the latter poem is also echoed elsewhere in some of the animal- and death-related poems: most notably, 'Catchollú'/'Incatation' and in these lines from 'Mise'/'Me':

> Fillfead air,   *I'll return to him,*
> Sé sin ormsa,   *that is, to me,*
> Ar leaba ár mbáis. *on our deathbed.*

Just as Yeats claimed that an artist faced a 'choice' between 'perfection of the life or of the work,'[33] Ó Ríordáin felt divided about the individual's need for company versus the need for solitude, contemplation, and thinking for one's self. Typically he had mixed and conflicting feelings about either choice, usually preferring one option from the vantage point of the other, so that the faraway hills were always the greener. In truth, he lived and fluctuated between the two. In 'Sos'/'Relief,' for example, it is as if he has actually gone to the 'dance at Billy Brennan's barn' (which Kavanagh shuns in 'Inniskeen Road: July Evening'[34]) but still finds no relief, returning once more to solitude and to the mirror of art from which some (temporary) 'peace,' it seems, is more likely to be derived. Which way to turn seems a constant question in Ó Ríordáin's oeuvre as far back as 'Ualach na beatha'/'The burden of life' where one group of learned authors point one way, and another group point the opposite way, leaving the poet in a state of painful indecision. In practice, he tentatively, intermittently followed the 'community' on the more travelled way of the church or Gaeltacht or 'people' but he would periodically turn his Joycean back and go his own lonely way, the private way of the artist, reflecting on both paths in dramatic, startling poems. His poems in this category range from 'Saoirse'/'Liberty' (where any apparent haughtiness on the part of the artist/speaker is counter-balanced by irony and a resigned acknowledgement that he necessarily shares the Metaphysical 'restlessness' of the human condition) to the moving empathy and unflinching *self*-criticism of 'An dán dúr'/'The dour poem' and 'Teip'/'Shortcoming.'

Ó Ríordáin's attitude towards women in his poetry is something of a vexed subject: Ní Dhomhnaill has noted how the refrain in Ó Ríordáin's 'Banfhile'/'Woman-poet'[35] repeats 'again and again with a sense of ever-increasing hysteria "Ní file ach filíocht an bhean" (Woman is not poet but poetry).' The poem concludes with the speculation that if women 'take to [writing] poetry,' they could soon 'produce off-spring' without any 'help from males,' and a man 'would be nothing,' not even 'a poet.' By post-1970s, post-feminism standards, the poem clearly voices disturbingly prescriptive and de-limiting ideas regarding gender roles. But is this a poem espousing sexism or more an expression of anxiety about declining male power (including the poet's own) and the rising, counter-balancing power of women (including women poets)? Notably, the poem was not published in any of Ó Ríordáin's collections during his lifetime. He read it in public in 1971, the same year that *Línte Liombó* was published, though it was not included in that volume; instead it was collected from among his papers and added to the posthumous collection, *Tar Éis mo Bháis*/After My Death (1978). To add to the uncertainty about just how far Ó Ríordáin (a fan of Emily Dickin-son and welcomer of Ní Dhomhnaill on the Irish poetry scene) actually believed the sexist notion that 'a woman is not a poet but poetry,' the poem seems to have its roots in a conversation with Gaeltacht poet 'An File' in which it was the latter who expressed such views while Ó Ríordáin, in fact, argued against them,[36] just as he had previously done in defending (as well as criticizing) Máire Mhac an tSaoi as a poet.[37] Perhaps this poem should be taken as a reminder that even though the 'I' of Ó Ríordáin's poetry (like Kava-nagh's) most often does seem to refer to the poet himself, it may (in some cases) be just *one* of his selves or *part* of himself. In the case of 'Banfhile'/'She-poet,' the author and/or speaker or persona is argu-ably most interested in playfully extending metaphors of artistic v. genetic 'creativity' into a Metaphysical-style conceit in the manner of John Donne. This could explain why the poem came to be written at all, while concern regarding its undemocratic credo may also account for the poet withholding the work from publication.[38]

When, for this current selection of Ó Ríordáin's poems, several women poets were each asked to choose and translate several of his poems, the request was met with universally positive, but also some qualified, responses: at least one poet said that, among other criteria, she did not want to tackle any poems that were 'ag caitheamh anuas ar na mná'/'speaking ill of women.' Most likely, she was thinking of the unfortunately long shadow cast by the poem 'Banfhile.' Yet, when Ó Ríordáin's other poems directly concerning women are considered together, including his eulogy of Eibhlín Dubh Ní Chonaill, 'Athmhúscailt na hóige'/'The reawakening of youth' (*Tar Éis mo Bháis*, p. 43), one finds a wider and more balanced representation of women in his work. Included in this selection, for example, are romantic, even sentimental, early love poems ('Cuireadh'/ 'Invitation'), others that powerfully image and register the devastation of lost love ('Ní raibh sí dílis'/'She was not faithful'), and even some late lyrics that display his modern and increasingly liberal sensibility regarding sexual morality ('Préachán'/'Crow' and 'Do striapach'/'To a prostitute'). In these latter poems, Ó Ríordáin seems finally to have leaned more towards the free-playing Joycean mode rather than any straight-laced Corkerian (or Catholic) orthodoxy.

One of the underestimated joys of Ó Ríordáin's oeuvre is his whole menagerie of animal poems, sometimes featuring his own brand of metamorphosis. In some of these poems (including 'An lacha'/'The duck' and 'Catchollú'/'Incatation'), he manages to step outside of himself ('the burden of me-ness') and to focus on something else, something external to himself just as he advocated (in the introduction to *Eireaball Spideoige* and repeatedly in his diary) as necessary for the individual and for poetry, too.[39] Yet even these poems bear the mark of one of Ó Ríordáin's 'masters,' namely Aesop,[40] and turn out to be just as anthropomorphic as his other animal poems. 'An lacha'/'The duck' and 'Catchollú'/'Incatation' ostensibly refer to the titular animals themselves but the poems also seem to reflect back on (or invite comparison with) human nature and society, as occurs more openly in the rein-biting satire of 'Tulyar' and erotic mystery of 'Na leamhain'/'The moths.'

Some of the animal poems consist of such close observation that the revelations within them seem to have profound implications regarding the nature of being, including for us as one more living and breathing creature sharing time and space in this one world: see, for example, 'Malairt'/'Switch' or 'An cat'/'The cat.' There's also an atmosphere of loneliness surrounding Ó Ríordáin's animal poems, a sense of isolation, a suggestion that animals were some-times his only (and sometimes his preferred) company. He seems especially to have felt a tremendous respect for creatures which truly 'selve,' which both sound and act as what they are, without pretension or hypocrisy. In his anarchic vision, human beings might be preferable, therefore, if they could have more of the innocence and honesty of animals, and could empathise more with them. This is part of the thinking behind poems such as 'Malairt'/'Switch' and diary entries such as this (my translation):

> I look at a bottle and I am bottled. I think of a woman and I am woman-ed. That is, the bottle and the woman raise me out of myself, remove the burden of 'me-ness.' I am turned into a bot-tle, a woman, just by thinking about them. A thought is a sort of magic wand. This flight [flexibility/movement] is necessary. You would go insane if you were always yourself. Life and self are multi-dimensional. We have to be bottles, horses, and prayers [etc.] or else we would go mad. A lunatic is someone who has tripped and fallen into himself and can't get out . . . And a lunatic is someone who has tripped and fallen into a bottle and can't get out. That's what it is. 'No Loitering.' A per-son must always keep travelling from self to self.[41]

Ó Ríordáin's poems directly about language include 'Na Blas-caodaí'/'The Blaskets' in which the poet is confident or, perhaps, optimistic about having a genuine source to tap into, one that will not let him (or 'us') down at least if we bother to tune into it. This poem is from his first collection, *Eireaball Spideoige* (1952), which was mostly well received (including for some of its artistic innovations and for being 'at a frontier of language'[42]) but was criticized on some counts, from some quarters, for occasionally using an 'unnatural' form of Irish, with neologisms and idiosyncratic agglutinations (such as 'focaldeoch'/'word-drink') that owed more, allegedly, to Gerard Manley Hopkins than to 'caint na ndaoine'/Irish as it is actually spoken, especially by native speakers. In some cases, Ó Ríordáin's early prosody was also questioned or criticised for occasionally owing too much, it was alleged, to the strong rhythms, possibly, of school-book poetry in English. Not surprisingly, Ó Ríordáin felt deeply stung by such criticism, which came from eminent figures in the Irish-language community, and echoed some of the condescension that the similarity self-taught Kavanagh encountered from comparable 'establishment' figures in the world of English-language literature in Ireland.

Ó Ríordáin was already his own harshest critic but was severely shaken by some of the more negative responses to a relatively small number of poems in a first collection featuring no fewer than *fifty-three* poems in all. One upshot of the criticism, however, was that he was thrown (for a long time) into confusion about his right and ability to write poetry at all and especially in Irish. However, this personal 'language issue' became one of the main subjects in his pared-down but strong second collection, *Brosna* (1964). The Irish language is addressed directly in 'A Ghaeilge im pheannsa'/'To the Irish in my pen,' with a barrage of questions that hint at some of the confusion Ó Ríordáin himself experienced. In another poem, Irish is a language only 'leath-liom'/'half-mine.' But, ironically, these poems of linguistic doubt are themselves replete with a rich ore derived from the poet's careful mining of deep seams of language that ran all the way back to his childhood, that were enhanced by his growing links with the Kerry Gaeltacht, and crowned by his reading of Irish-language literature (long past, recent and contemporary). All of this increasingly combined with his own Eliot-inspired 'individual talent' and internationally-informed aesthetics to the extent that, latterly, he could even make light of the by now wearisome topic of language in the salutary satire of 'Údar'/'Expert' or 'Author.'

For Ó Ríordáin, words were stones to be flung at death or doom; every sentence an assault against the death sentence.[43] Poetry, meanwhile, seemed to literally keep him going, to preserve sanity, memory and worth in a world where everything and everyone seem to be blown away by the wind into oblivion (images which recur throughout his work). For this reason, even his poems on the theme of 'death' are, in fact, as much about life and (what Sean O'Casey would call) the will to life: see 'Claustrophobia' where the poet-speaker holds out (even if it's just for one night more) the affirming flame of a 'Republic of light' in a world encroached upon by the forces of night. The poem 'Oíche Nollaig na mBan'/'Women's Christmas' suggests an acceptance of the inevitability of death and, to some extent, a sense of release and relief (not surprising, perhaps, for a long term veteran of TB); elsewhere, in 'Na fathaigh'/'The giants,' death is met with battling defiance. Most startling of all are the poems which find the words and images not just to describe but to give genuinely spooky intimations of near-death experiences and of witnessing, before time, one's own ghost-hood:

> In aice an fhíona
> tá coinneal is sceoin.
>
> *Next to the wine*
> *is a candle. And fear.*
>   —'Claustrophobia'
>
> Tá ceantar ag taisteal ón spéir,
> Tá comharsanacht suite ar mo mhéar.
>
> *A district is shooting from the sky,*
> *a neighbourhood poised on my finger.*
>   —'Fiabhras'/'Fever'

Chím chugam mé féin gan corp umam,
ach fós mo scáth 'om thionlacan.

I see myself approach, bodiless,
though my shadow follow on.
            —'An Gad is giorra don scornach'/
            'The noose nearest the neck'

To within three weeks of his death,[44] Ó Ríordáin kept account of his quest and questioning mind. In doing so he put himself and his existence unflatteringly and unflinchingly under the microscope of his art. But this was not mere self-obsession or navel-gazing. One of his literary heroes, Joyce, is said to have focussed on Dublin to 'get to the heart of all the cities in the world';[45] another, William Blake, famously concentrated on a grain of sand to see the world, and on a blade of grass to view the universe; finally, Ó Ríordáin's peer and contemporary Patrick Kavanagh honed in on the 'parish' in order to find the 'universal.'[46] Similarly, Ó Ríordáin often focussed on the 'I' of his own individual self but this was a way of reaching and reflecting upon the 'I' of each and every one of us, the 'duine aonair'/'lone individual' in isolation, in society and *vis à vis* society.[47] What he found was that the 'I' is, for good or ill, 'incorrigibly plural';[48] he also believed (influenced by St Augustine and Christian theology in general) that each individual, paradoxically, possesses some soul or essence which make him or her unique.[49] His poetry as a whole, however, concentrates more often on the *plurality* of self, on movement and change which both thrilled and frightened him but which he deemed to be essential to art and to active existence. Thus, we mostly find Ó Ríordáin 'forever travelling from me to me'[50] or 'hopping on a moving train' of time, selfhood and art itself. En route, he casts a wary (sometimes weary) eye on life, death and much in-between, improvising on his encounters with people and things, words and ideas, and (often) animals. His writings suggest that, spiritually, he was a hobo of the blues highway of mid-twentieth-century Ireland, like a

Woody Guthrie to the Dylans and Joni Mitchell who came next in the Irish pantheon of poets: from the *INNTI* generation to today's leading lights, including Biddy Jenkinson and Gearóid Mac Lochlainn. As with Guthrie's songs, Ó Ríordáin's poems continue to resonate in, and to reach beyond, his own cultural context.

Frank Sewell

ACKNOWLEDGMENTS

A huge debt of gratitude is owed to Professor Seán Ó Coileáin, academic, critic, and Ó Ríordáin's biographer, who generously shared valuable advice and insights. Not consulted on every word or phrase, Seán deserves credit for the translation 'successes' resulting from when he was consulted; and, equally, he deserves no blame for any inevitable instances when individual translators deemed it necessary or appropriate to take some liberties in translation.

Poet and critic Louis de Paor has been equally kind, and helpfully firm, in sharing his deep knowledge of Ó Ríordáin's individual writing style, a style which presents numerous challenges to any contemporary translator.

Finally, the translators who contributed to this text are to be commended for their craft, craftiness, and patience. No one is more aware than they are of both the difficulty and the fascination of translating poetry, or of the 'dream diúltaithe'/the 'rejected crowd' of alternatives for any single word, phrase, or line; alternatives that ultimately have to be dismissed in favour of one option or compromise only.

Ó Ríordáin once asked 'cén mise nó frithmhise / a chífí im scathán?' ('which me or counter-me / will be seen in my mirror?'). Hopefully, he would be reasonably satisfied with the versions of his poems which appear in this volume via the looking-glass of translation.

from Eireaball Spideoige *(1952)*

SEO LIBH A DHÁNTA TRÍD AN TÍR . . .

Seo libh a dhánta tríd an tír,
Ní mó ná sásta sinne libh,
Ach ba lú ná sin bhur sástacht linn,
Dá mb'eol díbh leath bhur n-ainnise.

Do cumadh sibh, a chlann véarsaí,
Is sinne ar easpa gramadaí,
Gan Institiúid gan eagnaí,
Gan ach comhairle eaglach ár gcroí
I lár na hoíche diamhaire.

Má castar libh fear léinn sa tslí,
Bhur rún ná ligidh leis, bhur sians,
Ní dá leithéid a cumadh sibh:
Tá baint agaibh le bualadh croí
Ar chuma an éinín bheannaithe.

ONWARD, POEMS, THROUGH THE LAND . . .

Onward, poems, through the land.
I'm no more satisfied with you
than you would ever be with me
if you knew half what's wrong with you.

My brood of verses, you were begot
when I was found wanting in grammar,
outside of Institutes and Orders,
with only my quaking heart as guide
deep in the mysteries of night.

Now if an expert crosses your path,
don't betray your song or secret.
Not designed for the likes of him,
you're on the side of the beating heart,
the same wing as the holy spirit.

trans. Frank Sewell

AN DALL SA STUDIO

'Suigh síos agus déanfaidh mé pictiúir díot,'
Adúrtsa leis an dall,
'Tá cathaoir id aice ansin sa chúinne,'
D'iompaigh sé a cheann,
Is do shín amach an lámh sin oilte ar chuardach,
Gach méar ag snámh go mall
Mar mhéaranna ceoltóra ar a uirlis,
Is bhí an uirlis ann:
Do sheinn sé ar an aer táin nótaí ciúnais,
Goltraí bog na ndall,
Na snámhaithe critheaglacha gur thuirling
Ar bhruach na habhann—
An suíochán sin a luas-sa leis, sa chúinne,
Is do shuigh sé ann.
Siúd láithreach é ag cíoradh a chuid gruaige,
Mo réice dall!

THE BLIND MAN IN THE STUDIO

'Sit down and I'll paint your portrait,'
I said to the blind man.
'There's a chair beside you in the corner.'
He turned his head
and stretched out his hand long used to searching,
every finger swimming slowly
like the fingers of a musician on his instrument,
and the instrument was there:
he played a fistful of quiet notes on the air,
a slow air of the blind,
until the fearful swimmers
landed on the bank of the chair
where he sat down
and straight away began combing his hair,
my blind rake!

trans. Peter Sirr

UALACH NA BEATHA

Is deacair an t-ualach seo d'iompar
    A thiomnaigh m'athair don chré,
Tráth ní raibh ann ach sciath ghliondair,
    Táim aga im chruiteachán fé.

Ní fuascailt dom braith ar na húdair,
    A mhúinfeadh an tslí do gach n-aon,
Is drong díobh ag cáineadh an chúrsa
    A mholann drong eile go tréan.

Tá comharthaí i mbéal an dá chúrsa
    Is scamaill as sin feadh a raon,
Scaipfidh gach scamall ach siúl tríd,
    Ach caithfear an bhreith thabhairt roimh ré.

Is minic bhraitheas milseacht i maighdean
    A fhág me go trochailte tréith,
A dhein síoraíocht gan faoiseamh den aimsir
    Is feitheamh dem ghníomhartha go léir.

Ach ba nimhní an mhilseacht sa chomhartha
    Ná slimchrot aon bhéithe fán spéir,
Ní haonchorp mná óige bhí romham ann
    Ach ilchorp na bantrachta féin.

Bhí aoibhneas gach mná dar luigh síos ann
    Is fiainmhian gach fir a saolaíodh,

THE BURDEN OF LIFE

I carry this gruelling burden
    that commended my father to his grave.
Once it was only a barrier to joy,
    but I am now this sickly hunch-back.

There's no redemption relying on authors
    who want to teach us the right way,
for one crowd condemns a path
    the other crowd strongly commends.

There are signs at the beginning of both paths,
    and clouds forming along each route,
clouds that scatter if you walk on through,
    but your choice must be made beforehand.

I've learned that the sweetness of a maiden
    leaves me feeling weak and worn-down,
and time becomes an anxious eternity,
    delaying all my actions.

But the image's sweetness was more painful
    than the slender-shape of any woman on earth.
It wasn't one woman's body before me
    but the embodiment of womanhood itself.

There was the joy of every female who lay down
    and wild desire born of every man born,

Bhí an buanordú seanda 'Méadaighidh!' ann,
Bhí ualach le roinnt ar mo dhroim.

Iar mbíogadh as aisling na feola
Tháinig fuaradh agus báine ar mo ghné;
Do scrúdaíos an dara ródchomhartha,
Cé go mb'fhonn liom éalú gan é léamh.

Ardchnoc is sneachta ar a bharr
Agus umhalmhachnamh uaigneach sa spéir,
Gaoth bhorb gan fothain mhná,
Staonadh agus cúngfhocal Dé.

Do theip orm teacht ar chruinnchomhairle
D'easpa an mhisnigh im chroí,
Do teilgeadh mé amach as na bóithre,
Agus fágadh mé caite cois claí.

the age-old command always to 'Multiply,'
    and the share of that burden was on my back.

After rousing from a dream of flesh,
    a coolness and a pallor came over me;
I studied the sign for the second path
    though I wanted to flee without reading it:

a mountain peak with snow on the summit
    and the humble reflection of loneliness in the sky;
such a bitter wind without the shelter of a woman,
    abstinence and the narrow word of God.

I failed to find any clear counsel
    for the absence of courage in my heart.
I was banished from both of the pathways,
    and left abandoned beside a ditch.

trans. Denise Blake

A SHEANFHILÍ, MÚINÍDH DOM GLAO

Tá focail ann dá mb'eol dom iad
Folaithe i gceo na haimsire,
Is táim ag cur a dtuairisc riamh
Ó chuir an ré an tsaint orm:
Táid scaipithe i leabhraibh léinn,
Is fós i gcuimhne seanóirí,
Is ag siúl na sráide im chuimhne féin,
Och, buailim leo is ní aithním iad.

Tá aisling ann, is is eol dom í,
Ag fiuchadh i mbroinn mo shamhlaíochta,
Lasair gheal gan chorp mar ghaoith,
Is corp oiriúnach á impí aici,
Abhar linbh í ag santú saoil,
Bean mé nach maighdean is nach máthair,
A sheanfhilí, múinídh dom glao
A mheallfadh corp dom shamhailtgharlach.

OLD POETS, TEACH ME THE CALL

There are words, if only I knew them,
hidden in the mist of time,
and I am always pursuing them
since the moon lit my desire:
they are scattered in learned tomes
and even in the memory of old men;
down the streets of my mind as I roam
I run into them without knowing them.

There is a vision, that I know well,
simmering in the womb of my imagination,
a bright flame without substance, a breath,
pleading for an appropriate shape,
this potential child, eager to be born.
I am a woman, neither virgin nor mother;
old poets, teach me the call
that will bring form to my imagined urchin.

trans. Colm Breathnach

BACAIGH

Im shiúlta tríd an saol
Nuair fhéachaim seal im thimpeall
Dar liom do chím i mbéal
An tsagairt tríd a dhiagacht,
Is i rosc an bhaitsiléir
Ná tadhallfadh bean le píce,
Is i ngliogaireacht na mbé
Lean ceard na geanmnaíochta,
Leamhchúthaileacht gan chéill
Na droinge sin bacaíochta
A shíneann lámh don déirc
Is ná labhrann focal choíche.

BEGGARS

In my journey through this life
as I look around
it seems to me I see
in the priest's pious mouth,
in the eye of the bachelor
who wouldn't touch a woman with a barge pole,
and in the cackling of women
who follow the trade of purity,
the meaningless simpering smile
of that crew of beggars
who stretch out their hands
and never say a word.

trans. Peter Sirr

NÍ RAIBH SÍ DÍLIS

Tá an tseana-Laoi ag urnaí soir,
    Is righin a paidir,
Is ré bhuí fhómhair clóbhuailte istigh
    I suaimhneas leathan
Na fiormaiminte, is solas lae
    I bhfanntais dheirg,
Is maidrín 'na luí go tréith
    I gcodladh meirbh.
Mo chroí dá dtomfainn ins an Laoi,
    San abhainn dheirg,
Do réabfadh sí mar scuaine diabhal
    Gach bruach le feirg.
Dá gcuirfinn smaoineamh i ngach néall,
    Mo smaointe buile,
Bheadh spéirling ifreannda sa spéir
    Is deamhain ar mire
Ag seiliú mallacht ar an ré
    Is ag cacadh tine,
Is an ghrian a rug léi solas lae
    Níor mhór di filleadh
Mar shárú ar an ngnáth-dhul-fé,
    Is urchóid ifrinn
A leathanfhógairt ins an spéir
    Le hiomad gile.
Dá ligfinn och dem bhrón i gcluais—
    Mo bhrón do-inste,

SHE WAS NOT FAITHFUL

The Lee flows east like an old prayer,
    an unbending psalm,
and a harvest moon is imprinted
    on the wide, stretched calm
of the firmament, the light of day
    collapsing in a red heap,
and a small dog is stretched out
    exhausted by the heat.
Were I to plunge my livid heart
    into the reddening river,
it would maraud from bank to bank
    like a company of devils.
If I sent a thought to every cloud
    straight from my turbulent mind
hell would be raging in the heavens
    and fiends of every kind
would spit their curses at the moon
    and shit out streams of fire;
the sun which had carried the light of day
    would be summoned, and required
to overcome its setting self
    and to proclaim hell's fire
and all its evil defeated
    by a sky filled with brightness.
Were I to whisper even a hint
    of my unutterable sorrow,

An mhaidrín 'na luí i suan
Do raghadh le díograis
Ag sealgaireacht i bpluaisibh bróin,
Ag lorg fola
An chogair líon a chroí d'anró
Is é ina chodladh.
'Nois canaim é mar shíorchurfá
Is bím go smaointeach
Á iompar liom ó áit go háit,
'Ní raibh sí dílis.'

The dog which has lain fast asleep
    would rouse itself to follow
and hunt its prey in gloomy caves
    to take its bloody revenge
on the awful whisper that filled its heart
    with foreboding while it slept.
Now I carry deep inside
    a burden like an old refrain,
bearing it here, bearing it there:
    she was not faithful.

trans. Paddy Bushe

AN PEACA

Thit réal na gealaí i scamallsparán,
 Go mall, mall, faitíosach,
Mar eala ag cuimilt an locha sa tsnámh,
 Is do chuimil go cneasta an oíche.

Do scéigh sí go tóin an scamallsparáin—
 Anam dea-chumtha na hoíche—
Mar chomhfhuaim ag titim go ceolmhar trí dhán,
 Is do chritheas le fuacht na filíochta.

Ach teilgeadh daoscarscread míchumtha ard
 'Na urchar trí ghloine na hoíche
Is cheapas go bhfaca na blúiríní fáin
 Fé chrúbaibh an mhasla san aoileach.

D'fhéachas arís ar lámhscríbhinn an dáin,
 Ach prós bhí in áit na filíochta—
An ré is na scamaill is an spéir mar ba ghnáth—
 Mar bhí peaca ar anam na hoíche.

THE SIN

A sixpenny bit of a moon dropped
    into a cloud-purse, so slowly, shyly,
like a swan brushing lake water in the swim,
    and gently brushed the night.

She edged to the bottom of the cloud-purse—
    a well-shaped soul of the night—
like assonance gliding through a poem,
    and I shivered under the chill of poetry.

But a loud, shapeless rabble-scream was hurled,
    smashing the glass of night,
and I thought I saw scattered shards
    under trotters of insult on a dunghill.

I looked again at the manuscript of the poem
    but it was prose instead of poetry—
the moon and the clouds and the sky as usual—
    because there was sin on the soul of the night.

trans. Noel Monahan

AN DOIRCHEACHT

Ag luí dhom im leaba anocht
Is daille na hoíche ar mo shúilibh
Smaoinim gan feirg gan tocht,
Gan oiread is deoir ar mo ghruannaibh,
Ar na soilse do múchadh im shaol:
Gach solas dar las ann do múchadh
Le tubaist dochreidte do shéid
Mar an ghaoth seo ag béicigh im chluasaibh.
Is ait liom gur mise an té
A chaill gach aon dóchas a fuair sé,
Is ait liom go rabhas-sa inné
Go dóchasach ainnis im bhuachaill,
Ach tá an doircheacht codlatach séimh,
Níl cúram ar bith ar mo shúilibh,
Is ní saoire ina buile an ghaoth
Ná an té tá gan solas le múchadh.

THE DARK

Lying in my bed tonight,
the blackness of night on my eyes,
I think without anger or emotion
or a single tear on my cheeks
of the lights that went out in my life:
every light that was lit was quenched
by unbelievable disaster that blew
like this wind screeching in my ears.
I find it strange that I lost
every hope that came my way,
I find it strange that only yesterday
I was the awkward hopeful boy;
but the dark of sleep is gentle,
my eyes are free from care,
and the wind is no freer in its frenzy
than the man with no light to quench.

trans. Peter Sirr

AN STOIRM

Tá an doras á chraitheadh is gan Críostaí ann
Ach gaoth dhall stuacach ag réabadh
Go liobarnach siar is aniar san oíche.
Tá a gúna á stracadh anonn is anall
Is á pholladh ag snáthaidí géara
Na fearthainne, atá ag titim 'na mílte.
Tá an tseanbhean fá chritheagla ag féachaint suas
Trí dhíon an tí, ag lorg Dé,
Is port gainmheach na fearthainne go diablaí thuas
Ag báitheadh an fhocail ar a béal.
Siúd léi go himníoch is coinneal 'na glaic
Ag daingniú na fuinneoige;
Nuair thit an solas coinnle ar an ngloine, las
Na ceathanna bolgóidí.
Do ghortaigh dealg fhuar fearthainne mo lámh,
D'fhéachas de gheit;
Braon duibh as an bpeann reatha dhein an smál,
Bheadh braon fearthainne glan.

THE STORM

The door is rattled and no Christian there
but a blind belligerent wind tearing
clumsily westward and back in the night.
Her dress dragged this way and that,
performed by sharp needles
of rain falling in their thousands.
Trembling with fear, the old woman looks up
through the roof of the house, for God,
while the rain's grating tune, like a devil above,
smothers the words on her lips.
There she goes, warily, clutching a candle,
securing the windows.
When the candlelight fell on the pane,
showers of bubbles lit up,
a freezing dart of rain stung my hand,
startled, I looked down:
a dark drop from the moving pen made the mark,
a drop of rain would be clear.

trans. Frank Sewell

CUIREADH

Ba mhaith liom tráthnóna do chaitheamh leat,
Is leoithne ag seinm id ghlór,
Tá staonadh na naomh i ngach peaca leat,
Is paidir diamhasla id bheol.

Ó, tar chugham tráthnóna is labhair liom,
Is mithid dom deoch díot a ól,
Ó, bí ar feadh oíche im ragairne,
Led mheiscese soilsigh mo ród,

Dein is cuir solas im dhearcaibhse
Is chífead dath géime na mbó;
Tar chugham is cloisfead gan bac ar bith
Rannaireacht rúnda na rós.

Ná fan riamh, a chuisle, rófhada uaim,
Mar scaipeann an mheisce mar cheo,
Is ní labhrann an abhainn thíos ach gramadach,
Is bímse chomh dall le dlíodóir.

INVITATION

I'd love to spend an evening with you,
a light air playing on your tongue,
the abstention of saints in each sin with you,
a blasphemous prayer on your lips.

Oh, come talk to me for an evening—
high time I drank my fill of you.
Oh, spend a night on the tear with me;
with your merriment light up my road.

Go on—enlighten my vision
and I'll see the colour of the cows' low.
Come to me and I'll hear without bother
the mysterious rhyming of the rose.

Don't stay away too long, my dear,
because joy disperses like mist
and the river below talks only grammar,
while I am as blind as a barrister.

trans. Celia de Fréine

AN DUAL

Beirt bhan óg ag trasnú sráide
Lámh ar láimh, iad uaim i gcéin,
Raideann bean díobh fialfholt álainn
Óna héadan siar 'na léim.

B'shin foltléim dar thugas grá riamh,
Léim a charas im shamhlaíocht,
Mar chomhartha áilleachta iomláine
Gan súil agam í d'fheiscint riamh.

Ná ní fhaca an radharc seo sráide,
Buaileadh sí-bhob ar mo shúil,
Ceann na mná sin a shiúil lámh léi
Bhí ag léimnigh mar bheadh dual.

Deireadh snasa cá bhfuil fáil air?
Bíonn geanc nó fiacail ann de shíor
Á choscadh díreach ar an dtáirseach,
Is druideann radharc na bhFlaitheas siar.

LOCKS

Two young women crossing a street
hand in hand, away in the distance.
One flings her veil of lovely hair
back from her brow with a flounce.

I always loved that flouncing hair,
so dear that it sprang to mind
like a symbol of the Beautiful
that I never thought I'd find.

Nor did I see this street-vision,
a fairy-trick deceived my eyes:
the head of hair bouncing along
was the woman's she walked beside.

Where can total perfection be found?
There's always a wonky nose or teeth
barring it right there at the threshold,
and the vision of Heaven recedes.

trans. Eilish Martin and Frank Sewell

SOS

Mar sceach fé thathaint na gaoithe
Tá m'anam á lúbadh anocht,
 Thiar ná thoir níl dídean
 Mar is poll im cheann gach smaoineamh
 Trína liúnn an ghaoth gan sos.

Raghad go halla an rince
Mar a mhúineann fuaimint cos
 Is béarlagar na mianta
 Bodhaire seal don intinn,
 Is gheobhad ansan mo shos.

Ach do labhair gach aghaidh go líofa,
Ach m'aghaidhse bhí i dtost,
 I dteanga nár airíos-sa
 Á labhairt amuigh san iasacht
 'Na mbím go haonarach.

Cumfad féin de bhriathra
Scáthán véarsaí anocht,
As a labharfaidh aghaidh scoraíochtach
A mhalartóidh liom faoistin,
 Is gheobhad ansan mo shos.

RELIEF

Like a thorn-bush battered by the wind,
my soul is twisted and turned tonight;
west or east, there's no shelter,
every thought a hole in the head
the wind howls through without relief.

I will go along to the dance-hall
where the sound of stamping feet
and the code words of desire
will numb the mind a while,
and then I'll find some relief.

But every face, except mine
which was silent, spoke fluently
in a tongue I'd never heard
out in the wilderness
where I exist alone.

Tonight, I will craft from words
a looking-glass of verse
where a neighbourly face will speak
and exchange confession with me,
then I'll find some relief.

trans. Robert Welch and Frank Sewell

ÉIST LE FUAIM NA HABHANN

Do chuamar ag siúlóid san oíche,
    Bean agus triúr fear,
Agus bhí an abhainn ag labhairt léi féin gan faoiseamh,
    Agus cé nár thuigeas a leath
Dob eol dom go raibh sí lándáiríre
    Agus dob eol dom nár chleas
Aon bhraon amháin dá briathra
    Ach uiscechomhrá glan.

Ach do scaipeas-sa easpa céille
    Tríd an oíche gan stad,
Agus do chaitheas púicín ró-aerach
    De bhriathra gan mhaith
Ar aghaidh m'anama go bréagach
    Ag dalladh beirte lem ais
Sara bhfeicidís na deargchréachta,
    Sara gcloisidís an chnead.

Ach anois ó táim im aonar
    Bíodh m'anam lom gan bhrat,
Is labharfad fíor liom féinig
    Mar a labhair an abhainn gan chleas
Nuair a ardaigh dán go sléibhte
    Lena huisce féin ar fad,
Nuair nár ghéill do cheol an éithigh
    Ach lomuisceachas do chan.

LISTEN TO THE RIVER SPEAK

We went out walking in the night,
    a woman and three men,
the river babbling away to itself,
    and though I did not understand the half of it
I knew it was wholly in earnest—
    I knew there was no false note
in all that flow of talk,
    those waterwords clean and clear.

I was spouting my foolishness
    into the night without cease,
wearing a flippant mask,
    of words without worth,
false on the face of my soul;
    dazzling the two beside me
so they would not see my gaping wounds,
    would not hear me groaning.

But now that I walk alone,
    let my soul go bare and uncovered;
I will speak to myself
    as the river spoke, undeceiving,
when it rose a poem to the mountains
    in its own weight of water,
spurning the false music
    with its own clear voice.

trans. Theo Dorgan

CLÁIRSEACH SHEAN NA NGNÁTHRUD

Tioc, tioc, tioc, ar chearcaibh ghlaoigh,
  Is do tuigeadh domsa láithreach
Gur dán na focail tioc, tioc, tioc,
  De bhrí go bhfuilid ársa.

Is féidir seinnt mar Orpheus
  Ar chláirseach shean na ngnáthrud,
Tá uaigneas seanda ins an gcat
  Á ghoradh féin gan náire.

Mar do hairíodh an macalla sin
  I gcloignibh gan áireamh—
An caitín muinteartha ina luí
  Go drúiseach ar thinteánaibh.

Is titim siar go leanbach
  Im óige chlúracánach
Nuair a déantar fuarchorpán dem chois
  Le codladh grifín na snáthad.

Tá seanchas sa dúiseacht sin,
  Sa ghigilteas uafásach,
Is púcaí na mbéaloideasaí
  Mar shamhlaíos iad im pháiste.

THE VENERABLE HARP OF THE MUNDANE

Chuck, chuck, chuck, I summoned the hens
    and it came to me out of the air
that *chuck, chuck, chuck* are the words of a poem
    by having been always there,

and I can pluck like Orpheus
    the venerable harp of the mundane,
like the cat's age-old loneliness
    as she warms herself without shame.

Because that echo has been heard
    in an infinite number of heads—
the friendly wee cat stretched
    lasciviously, with the hearth for a bed.

And I slip back childishly
    to the tiny toddler I was
whenever, numbed by pins-and-needles,
    my leg freezes up like a corpse.

There's lore in that sudden sensation,
    in the unbearable tingling
and pookas straight out of folktales
    as I imagined them when young.

Ag sin trí téada luaite agam
    Ar chláirseach shean na ngnáthrud,
Gnáthghlaoch ar chearcaibh, cat ar lic,
    Is codladh grifín na snáthad.

That's three strings I've touched upon
    the ancient harp of familiar things:
calling the hens, a cat on the hearth
    and the numbness of pins-and-needles.

trans. Paddy Bushe

DO DHOMHNALL Ó CORCORA

Éirigh is can ár mbuíochas croí dhó,
Do mhúin sé an tslí,
Do dhúisigh eilit ár bhfilíochta
I gcoillte blian.

Do dhein dá anam cluas le héisteacht,
Is d'éist gan trua
(Dó féin, ná d'éinne mhúnlaigh véarsa),
Gur thit anuas

De phlimp ar urlár gallda an lae seo
Eoghan béal binn,
Aindrias mac Craith, Seán Clárach, Aodhgán,
Cioth filí.

Do leag méar chiúin ar chuislinn Aodhgáin,
Do chreid a luas,
Do gheal an lá ar intinn aosta
Dúinn ba dhual.

D'fhill sé leo an bhuíon filí seo
An staighre suas,
Is do shiúil sé bóithre lán de Mhuimhnigh,
É féin 's Eoghan Rua.

Do ghoid sé uathu cluas an chine,
Cluas spailpín,

FOR DANIEL CORKERY

Arise and sing our heart-full thanks
for he showed us the way.
He awakened the doe of poetry
asleep in the forest of years.

His soul became a listening ear
and he listened without pity
(to himself or to any poet's verse)
until there dropped down

in a plump on our Anglicized earth,
a shower of poets:
Eoghan of the sweet mouth,
Aindrias Mac Craith, Seán Clárach, Aodhgán.

He placed a placid finger on Aodhgán's pulse,
trusted his swiftness,
and day brightened on an ancient mind
that was native to us.

He followed this band of poets
upwards on their stairway,
and walked the roads of Munster
alongside Eoghan Rua

He carried away the native ear,
the ear of the spalpeen,

Níor fhulaing dán ar bith a thuilleadh
Ach gin gan teimheal.

Braithim é gan sos ag éisteacht
Mar athchoinsias;
Tá smacht a chluaise ar lúth mo véarsa,
Trom an chuing.

Tráthnóna na teangan in Éirinn,
Is an oíche ag bogthitim mar scéal,
D'éist sé le creagar i véarsa,
Is do chuala croí cine soiléir.

as he couldn't bear a tortuous verse,
only a poem born pure.

I know he is always with me,
listening as a second conscience,
controlling the flow of my verse.
The harness is heavy.

Late evening for the language in Ireland,
with night falling softly as a story,
he listened for the cricket in our poetry,
and heard the heart of the people.

trans. Denise Blake

ROITHLEÁN

Bhí ceol na hoíche seinnte
Is cnead na maidne im chluais
Nuair do rugas-sa mo ghreim docht
Ar urla bheag den suan,
A chlúdaigh m'anam thuas
I gceantar na míorúilt
San oíche mhór ealaíonta
'Na rinceann treabh na dtaibhreamh
Le ceolta míréasúin
Anonn is anall gan chúis.

Do choinníos uirthi greim docht,
An urla bheag dem shuan,
Lena sníomh i bhfoirm taibhrimh
Ach bhí an mhaidinchnead im chluais,
Is bhí an urla bheag róchúng,
Is níor shníomhas ach an tús,
Nuair do chas an tús sin timpeall
Gan trócaire ina roithleán:
    Do bheinn im ghealt go buan
    Ach gur scaoileas uaim an suan.

WHIRL

Night-music had drawn to a close
and morning whispered in my ear
when I laid firm hold on
a little wisp of sleep
that clothed my soul up there
in the miracle zone
of the great firmament
reeling to the dream-plough
illogically lilting
back and forth for no cause.

I held it firm as firm could be,
my little wisp of sleep,
that I might spin a dream thereof,
but morning whispered in my ear,
and the wisp was next to nothing.
All I had spun was the beginning
whereupon it turned about me
mercilessly whirling:
    had I not let slip that little sleep
    I would be forever moonstruck.

trans. Ciaran Carson

AN CAT

An cat d'fhágáil amuigh
    Sa chaochoíche leis féin,
Is an spéir ró-ard mar thigh,
    Ní dhéanfainn a leithéid.

Dhá shúil mar dhá thoitín
    I dtóin na hoíche i gcéin,
Is sceon i gcroí chaitín,
    Ní dhéanfainn a leithéid.

Féasóga cíortha ag crith
    Is ionga troda réidh,
Iontaoibh phiscín a lot,
    Ní dhéanfainn a leithéid.

Mar d'ólas smaointe an chait,
    Is d'fhair an cat go géar
Na smaointe im shúil ag teacht,
    Is d'fhásamar araon.

Do deineadh díom leathchat,
    Ba dhuine an cat dá réir,
An caidreamh a scoilt,
    Ní dhéanfainn a leithéid.

THE CAT

Leave the cat outdoors
    alone in the eyeless night,
under the sky's pitched height—
    I would never do that.

Two eyes cigarette-bright
    faraway in the deep dark,
its little cat-heart afright—
    I could never do that.

Combed whiskers twitching,
    and claws drawn for a fight.
Kittenish trust turned to spite—
    I would never do that.

For I took in the cat's mind,
    and the cat watched tight
my mind sliding into sight,
    and we both gained together.

I turned half-cat alright;
    so too the cat turned man.
Break up a kinship that tight?
    I could never do that.

Gráin sinsearach na gcat
Don chine daonna féin
'Na shúile siúd a bhrath—
    Do bheinn go brách i bpéin.

An ancient feline hatred
for the human race alight
in his eyes: to sense that
    would torment me day and night.

trans. Mary O'Donoghue

ADHLACADH MO MHÁTHAR

Grian an Mheithimh in úllghort,
    Is siosarnach i síoda an tráthnóna,
Beach mhallaithe ag portaireacht
    Mar screadstracadh ar an nóinbhrat.

Seanalitir shalaithe á léamh agam,
    Le gach focaldeoch dar ólas
Pian bhinibeach ag dealgadh mo chléibhse,
    Do bhrúigh amach gach focal díobh a dheoir féin.

Do chuimhníos ar an láimh a dhein an scríbhinn,
    Lámh a bhí inaitheanta mar aghaidh,
Lámh a thál riamh cneastacht seana-Bhíobla,
    Lámh a bhí mar bhalsam is tú tinn.

Agus thit an Meitheamh siar isteach sa Gheimhreadh,
    Den úllghort deineadh reilig bhán cois abhann,
Is i lár na balbh-bháine i mo thimpeall
    Do liúigh os ard sa tsneachta an dúpholl,

Gile gearrachaile lá a céad chomaoine,
    Gile abhlainne Dé Domhnaigh ar altóir,
Gile bainne ag sreangtheitheadh as na cíochaibh,
    Nuair a chuireadar mo mháthair, gile an fhóid.

Bhí m'aigne á sciúirseadh féin ag iarraidh
    An t-adhlacadh a bhlaiseadh go hiomlán,

MY MOTHER'S BURIAL

The June sun on the apple orchard,
    a rustle in the silk of gloaming, the interminable hymn
of an irritable bumblebee
    piercing the evening's scrim.

I'm reading a grubby old letter.
    With every word-sip a spear
of sorrow piercing my ribcage.
    Each word wringing out its own particular tear.

I'm thinking of the hand that wrote the letter.
    A hand as distinctive as any face.
A hand that had a Biblical charitableness.
    A hand healing the sick child with a herb of grace.

Now June fell back into mid-winter,
    the orchard was a white churchyard by a stream.
In the midst of the mute, all-surrounding snow
    was a black hole from which issued a scream.

The brightness of a young girl at her First Communion.
    The brightness of a host on the altar of God.
The brightness of milk spurting from a woman's breast.
    The brightness, when they buried my mother, of the very sod.

I was beating my brains in an attempt
    to fully taste the occasion when there flew

Nuair a d'eitil tríd an gciúnas bán go míonla
  Spideog a bhí gan mhearbhall gan scáth:

Agus d'fhan os cionn na huaighe fé mar go mb'eol di
  Go raibh an toisc a thug í ceilte ar chách
Ach an té a bhí ag feitheamh ins an gcomhrainn,
  Is do rinneas éad fén gcaidreamh neamhghnách.

Do thuirling aer na bhFlaitheas ar an uaigh sin,
  Bhí meidhir uafásach naofa ar an éan,
Bhíos deighilte amach ón diamhairghnó im thuata,
  Is an uaigh sin os mo chomhair in imigéin.

Le cumhracht bróin do folcadh m'anam drúiseach,
  Thit sneachta geanmnaíochta ar mo chroí,
Anois adhlacfad sa chroí a deineadh ionraic
  Cuimhne na mná d'iompair mé trí ráithe ina broinn.

Tháinig na scológa le borbthorann sluasad,
  Is do scuabadar le fuinneamh an chré isteach san uaigh,
D'fhéachas-sa treo eile, bhí comharsa ag glanadh a ghlúine,
  D'fhéachas ar an sagart is bhí saoltacht ina ghnúis.

Grian an Mheithimh in úllghort,
  Is siosarnach i síoda an tráthnóna,
Beach mhallaithe ag portaireacht
  Mar screadstracadh ar an nóinbhrat.

through the stilly brightness
    a robin, unruffled, completely without rue.

It would hang about the grave as if it understood
    the reason why it had come might slip
the minds of all but the one waiting in the coffin.
    I envied them their uncommon fellowship.

The air of Heaven came down on the grave.
    About the bird was a tremendous saintly glee.
I felt shut out of the mystery, a layman,
    while the grave itself kept its distance from me.

My concupiscent soul was wreathed in a sorrow-scent.
    The snow of chastity fell on my heart. Now I'm making room
in that selfsame, steadfast heart
    for one who carried me for nine months in her womb.

The gravediggers came with a terrific clanking
    of shovels and hurled
earth into earth. I turned away. A neighbour brushing his knee.
    I turned to the priest. The face of a man of the world.

The June sun on an apple orchard,
    a rustle in the silk of gloaming, the interminable hymn
of an irritable bumblebee
    piercing the evening's scrim.

Ranna beaga bacacha á scríobh agam,
    Ba mhaith liom breith ar eireaball spideoige,
Ba mhaith liom sprid lucht glanta glún a dhíbirt,
    Ba mhaith liom triall go deireadh lae go brónach.

They're so limp and lame, these stanzas I'm writing.

I'd like to grasp the robin's tail. As for those brushing clay from their knees, I'd like to brush them off completely.

However heavy-heartedly, I'd just like to get through this day.

trans. Paul Muldoon

NA FATHAIGH

Thuirling pianta diaidh ar ndiaidh,
    Pian ar phéin,
Níl sa chiapadh ach neamhní,
    Dúrt liom féin.

Tiocfaidh faoiseamh leis an ngréin,
    D'éirigh grian,
Lean mo bhroid ag dul i méid,
    Faire, a Chríost.

Lean na pianta ag argóint,
    Mise an t-abhar,
Focal níl sa phianfhoclóir
    Ná rabhas ann.

Iad am ithe, iad am ól,
    Iad am chrú,
Mé go béasach cneasta leo,
    Mé go humhal.

Ba leosan do chuaigh an lá,
    Mise a chaill,
Namhaid im thigh, an fhoighne is fearr,
    Tiocfaidh faill.

Fan, do chuaigh na pianta thar fóir,
    D'éiríos as,

THE GIANTS

The pains came down one by one,
    wave after wave of them.
I can hack this. This is nothing,
    I tell myself.

Morning will bring ease.
    The sun came up,
my distress just got worse.
    Oh, Christ, watch out.

The pains kept on arguing,
    with me as their subject.
In the lexicon of pain,
    I've gone through every word.

They've chewed my flesh and sucked
    the sap from my veins,
and me the well-mannered host,
    humble and meek.

They have won the day.
    I'm lost.
The enemy is in the house. Patience,
    and I'll wait my chance.

No. The pains have gone too far.
    But as I surrendered,

Léim mo sprid le gliondar mór,
    Lig sí scread.

In aghaidh Dé do lig sí scread,
    Dúshlán fé!
Scaoileadh sé gach pian 'na ghlaic,
    Táimse réidh.

Thuirling milseacht tríd an aer,
    Thuirling neart,
Chonac na fathaigh taobh le taobh,
    Dia is an scread.

my soul leapt in wonder
    and let out a scream.

A scream against God.
    Do your worst!
Let loose every pain in your armoury.
    I'm ready.

Solace was what descended
    from above, and strength.
I saw two giants side by side.
    The scream and God.

trans. Mary O'Malley

CÚL AN TÍ

Tá Tír na nÓg ar chúl an tí,
    Tír álainn trína chéile,
Lucht ceithre chos ag siúl na slí
    Gan bróga orthu ná léine,
    Gan Béarla acu ná Gaeilge.

Ach fásann clóca ar gach droim
    Sa tír seo trína chéile,
Is labhartar teanga ar chúl an tí
    Nár thuig aon fhear ach Aesop,
    Is tá sé siúd sa chré anois.

Tá cearca ann is ál sicín,
    Is lacha righin mhothaolach,
Is gadhar mór dubh mar namhaid sa tír
    Ag drannadh le gach éinne,
    Is cat ag crú na gréine.

Sa chúinne thiar tá banc dramhaíl'
    Is iontaisí an tsaoil ann,
Coinnleoir, búclaí, seanhata tuí,
    Is trúmpa balbh néata,
    Is citeal bán mar ghé ann.

Is ann a thagann tincéirí
    Go naofa, trína chéile,
Tá gaol acu le cúl an tí,

THE BACK OF THE HOUSE

At the back of the house is the Land of Youth,
a beautiful, untidy land,
where four-footed folk wend their way,
without shoes or shirt,
without English or Irish.

But a cloak grows on every back
in this untidy land,
and a language is spoken at the back of the house,
that no man knew but Aesop,
and he is in the clay now.

There are hens there and a clutch of chickens,
and a sluggish unsophisticated duck
and a great black dog like a foe in the land,
snarling at everybody,
and a cat milking the sun.

At the western corner is a bank of refuse,
containing the wonders of the world,
a chandelier, buckles, an old straw hat,
a trumpet dumb but elegant,
and a white goose-like kettle.

It is hither the tinkers come,
saintly and untidy,
they are germane to the back of the house,

Is bíd ag iarraidh déirce
Ar chúl gach tí in Éirinn.

Ba mhaith liom bheith ar chúl an tí
    Sa doircheacht go déanach
Go bhfeicinn ann ar chuairt gealaí
    An t-ollaimhín sin Aesop
    Is é ina phúca léannta.

and they are accustomed to beg
at the back of every house in Ireland.

I would wish to be at the back of the house,
when it is dark and late,
that I might see on a moonlight visit
the tiny professor Aesop,
that scholarly sprite.*

trans. Seán Ó Ríordáin

*Editor's note: Writing in the 1950s, Ó Ríordáin translated 'púca' as 'fairy' but, since then, various writers and critics have convincingly cast doubt upon the aptness of the changing term 'fairy' as a translation for the more trickster-like 'pooka.' The latter is here translated as 'sprite,' an entity which shares some of the ambiguity and unpredictability of a pooka, and some of the wit, playfulness, and even 'spirit' of Aesop himself.

MALAIRT

'Gaibh i leith,' arsa Turnbull, 'go bhfeice tú an brón
    I súilibh an chapaill,
Dá mbeadh crúba chomh mór leo sin fútsa bheadh brón
    Id shúilibh chomh maith leis.'

Agus b'fhollas gur thuig sé chomh maith sin an brón
    I súilibh an chapaill,
Is gur mhachnaigh chomh cruaidh air gur tomadh é fá
      dheoidh
    In aigne an chapaill.

D'fhéachas ar an gcapall go bhfeicinn an brón
    'Na shúilibh ag seasamh,
Do chonac súile Turnbull ag féachaint im threo
    As cloigeann an chapaill.

D'fhéachas ar Turnbull is d'fhéachas air fá dhó
    Is do chonac ar a leacain
Na súile rómhóra bhí balbh le brón—
    Súile an chapaill.

SWITCH

'Come over here,' said Turnbull, 'till you see the sorrow
    in the horse's eyes.
Had you such heavy hooves as these for feet there would be
      sorrow
    in your eyes too.

And it was plain to me, that he'd realised the sorrow
    in the horse's eyes so well,
So deeply had he contemplated it, that he was steeped
    in the horse's mind.

I looked at the horse, that I might see the sorrow
    standing in its eyes,
And saw instead the eyes of Turnbull looking at me
    from the horse's head.

I looked at Turnbull, then I took a second look,
    and saw looming from his face
The over-big eyes that were dumb with sorrow—
    the horse's eyes.

trans. Ciaran Carson

CNOC MELLERÍ

Sranntarnach na stoirme i Mellerí aréir
Is laethanta an pheaca bhoig mar bhreoiteacht ar mo
      chuimhne,
Laethanta ba leapacha de shonaschlúmh an tsaoil
Is dreancaidí na drúise iontu ag preabarnaigh ina mílte.

D'éirigh san oíche sidhe gaoithe coiscéim,
Manaigh ag triall ar an Aifreann,
Meidhir, casadh timpeall is rince san aer,
Bróga na manach ag cantaireacht.

Bráthair sa phroinnteach ag riaradh suipéir,
Tost bog ba bhalsam don intinn,
Ainnise naofa in oscailt a bhéil,
Iompar mothaolach Críostaí mhaith.

Do doirteadh steall anchruthach gréine go mall
Trí mhúnla cruiceogach fuinneoige,
Do ghaibh sí cruth manaigh ó bhaitheas go bonn
Is do thosnaigh an ghrian ag léitheoireacht.

Leabhar ag an manach bán namhdach á léamh,
Go hobann casachtach an chloig,
Do múchadh an manach bhí déanta de ghréin
Is do scoilteadh an focal 'na phloic.

MOUNT MELLERAY

The snore-snortle of a storm in Mount Melleray last night
brought back days of concupiscence hanging over me like a
        disease,
days that were featherbeds in which I would luxuriate
and lusts would hop around like so many fleas.

There arose in the night the footfalls of a fairy wind
as the Cistercians made their way to Mass,
so merrily, with their own hop, skip and a jump,
their sandals chanting psalms as monk after monk would pass.

A brother in the refectory, readying the dinner.
A silence that would have sufficed
as balm for any soul. A holy penury in his open mouth.
His unsophisticated demeanour befitting a follower of Christ.

A shapeless splash of sunlight that had slowly poured
through a conical window now avowed
its having taken the form of a monk.
The sun began to read aloud.

This white-robed cantankerous monk went on reading his book
till, out of nowhere, a bell had a coughing fit.
The monk composed of sunlight was just as suddenly snuffed.
The words in his cheeks were just as suddenly split.

Buaileadh clog Complin is bhrostaigh gach aoi
Maolchluasach i dtreo an tséipéil;
Bhí beatha na naomh seo chomh bán le braitlín
Is sinne chomh dubh leis an daol.

Allas ar phaidrín brúite im láimh,
Mo bhríste dlúth-tháite lem ghlúin,
Ghluais sochraid chochallach manach thar bráid,
Ba shuarach leat féachaint a thabhairt.

Ach d'fhéachas go fiosrach gan taise gan trua
Mar fhéachadar Giúdaigh fadó
Ar Lazarus cúthail ag triall as an uaigh
Is géire na súl thart á dhó.

Do thiteadar tharainn 'na nduine is 'na nduine,
Reilig ag síorphaidreoireacht,
Is do thuirling tiubhscamall de chlúimh liath na cille
Go brónach ar ghrua an tráthnóna.

'Tá an bás ag cur seaca ar bheatha anseo,
Aige tá na manaigh ar aimsir,
Eisean an tAb ar a ndeineann siad rud,
Ar a shon deinid troscadh is treadhanas.

'Buachaill mar sheanduine meirtneach ag siúl,
Masla ar choimirce Dé,
An té 'dhéanfadh éagóir dá leithéid ar gharsún
Do chuirfeadh sé cochall ar ghréin;

The bell for Compline had sounded and everyone hastened
along the beaten track
to the chapel. The lives of the saints were white as a sheet
while ours were beetle-black.

There was sweat on the rosary in my hand.
My trousers were stuck to my knees. To have touched the hem
of one of these hooded monks slowly filing by
would have been as inappropriate as to stare at them.

And stare I did, with a pitiless gaze,
as the Jews
must have stared at Lazarus coming, bashfully, from his grave,
their eyes burning him through and through.

One after another the monks would pass
like a graveyard praying a blue streak
and a thick cloud of mildew or verdigris from the church
fell sadly on the evening's cheek.

'Death holds this place in his icy grip.
The monks are in his service. He's their ball and chain.
He is the Abbot whom they obey.
It's for Death's sake they fast and abstain.

'To have a boy hobbling along like a feeble old man
is an abuse of God's protection. Anyone who's done
the likes of this to a boy
would think nothing of putting a cowl on the sun;

'Do scaipfeadh an oíche ar fud an mheán lae,
Do bhainfeadh an teanga den abhainn,
Do chuirfeadh coir drúise in intinn na n-éan
Is do líonfadh le náire an domhan.

'Tá an buachaill seo dall ar an aigne fhiain
A thoirchíonn smaointe éagsúla
Gan bacadh le hAb ná le clog ná le riail
Ach luí síos le smaoineamh a dhúile.

'Ní bhlaisfidh sé choíche tréanmheisce mná
A chorraíonn mar chreideamh na sléibhte,
'Thug léargas do Dante ar Fhlaitheas Dé tráth,
Nuair a thuirling na haingil i riocht véarsaí,'

Sin é dúirt an ego bhí uaibhreach easumhal,
Is é dallta le feirg an tsaoil,
Ach do smaoiníos ar ball, is an ceol os ár gcionn,
Gur mó ná an duine an tréad.

D'fhéachas laistiar díom ar fhásach mo shaoil,
Is an paidrín brúite im dhóid,
Peaca, díomhaointeas is caiteachas claon,
Blianta urghránna neantóg.

'would think nothing of spreading midnight over noon,
of trying to tame
the river's tongue, of assigning impure thoughts to birds,
of filling the world with a sense of shame.

'This boy has no sense of the unfettered mind
in which the seeds of certain ideas are sown,
heedless of Abbot, bell and Rule,
of the mind given over to its desires alone.

'The power of a woman who can move
mountains as surely as faith is one in which he'll never be
            immersed.
It was such a woman who afforded Dante a vision of Paradise
in which even the angels were strictly versed.'

That's how the ego weighed in, so full of itself,
so blinded by life that's out of control,
though it struck me later, while the music hung over us,
how the flock triumphs over a single soul.

I looked back at the waste of my life,
the rosary clenched in my fist,
at the years of sin, sloth, idleness,
the wilderness years from which only black nettles persist.

D'fhéachas ar bheatha na manach anonn,
D'aithníos dán ar an dtoirt,
Meadaracht, glaine, doimhinbhrí is comhfhuaim,
Bhí m'aigne cromtha le ceist.

Do bhlaiseas mórfhuascailt na faoistine ar maidin,
Aiseag is ualach ar ceal,
Scaoileadh an t-ancaire, rinceas sa Laidin,
Ba dhóbair dom tuirling ar Neamh.

Ach do bhlaiseas, uair eile, iontaoibh asam féin,
Mo chuid fola ar fiuchadh le neart,
Do shamhlaíos gur lonnaigh im intinn Spiorad Naomh
Is gur thiteadar m'fhocail ó Neamh.

Buarach ar m'aigne Eaglais Dé,
Ar shagart do ghlaofainn coillteán,
Béalchráifeacht an Creideamh, ól gloine gan léan,
Mairfeam go dtiocfaidh an bás!

Manaigh mar bheachaibh ag fuaimint im cheann,
M'aigne cromtha le ceist,
Nótaí ag rothaíocht anonn is anall,
Deireadh le Complin de gheit.

I looked at the life of that monk over there
and the idea of a verse immediately found me out—
the strictness, the clean lines, the depth, the little chimes
        here and there—
and I was burdened by doubt.

I'd tasted the great lightening of confession that morning,
renewal, the lifting of a weight.
The anchor was let slip, I danced in the Latin,
I almost landed at the Pearly Gates.

At another time I tasted something like self-reliance,
my blood boldly running its course,
and I imagined the Holy Spirit in my mind
giving my words a heavenly force.

But the Church itself was like a straw-rope hobble on a beast.
I would proclaim a man of the cloth
a eunuch, the Faith mere lip service. I'd drink a glass without
        remorse,
live life to the full before shuffling off.

The monks like bees were still buzzing in my head,
my mind still laden with qualms,
the notes of music turning over this way and that,
when there came an abrupt end to the Compline psalms.

Sranntarnach na stoirme i Mellerí aréir
Is laethanta an pheaca bhoig mar bhreoiteacht ar mo
      chuimhne
Is na laethanta a leanfaidh iad fá cheilt i ndorn Dé,
Ach greim fhir bháite ar Mhellerí an súgán seo filíochta.

The snore-snortle of a storm in Mount Melleray last night
bringing back days of concupiscence like a disease hanging
over me
and the days after those hidden in God's grasp
while I hold on tight to Mount Melleray with this straw-rope
of poetry.

trans. Paul Muldoon

OÍCHE NOLLAIG NA MBAN

Bhí fuinneamh sa stoirm a éalaigh aréir,
    Aréir oíche Nollaig na mBan,
As gealt-teach iargúlta tá laistiar den ré
    Is do scréach tríd an spéir chughainn 'na gealt,
Gur ghíosc geataí comharsan mar ghogallach gé,
    Gur bhúir abhainn shlaghdánach mar tharbh,
Gur múchadh mo choinneal mar bhuille ar mo bhéal
    A las 'na splanc obann an fhearg.

Ba mhaith liom go dtiocfadh an stoirm sin féin
    An oíche go mbeadsa go lag
Ag filleadh abhaile ó rince an tsaoil
    Is solas an pheaca ag dul as,
Go líonfaí gach neomat le liúrigh ón spéir,
    Go ndéanfaí den domhan scuaine scread,
Is ná cloisfinn an ciúnas ag gluaiseacht fám dhéin,
    Ná inneall an ghluaisteáin ag stad.

WOMEN'S CHRISTMAS

There was power in the storm that escaped last night,
    last night on Women's Christmas,
from the desolate madhouse behind the moon
    and screamed through the sky at us, lunatic,
making neighbours' gates screech like geese
    and the hoarse river roar like a bull,
quenching my candle like a blow to the mouth
    that sparks a quick flash of rage.

I'd like if that storm would come again,
    a night I'd be feeling weak
coming home from the dance of life
    and the light of sin dwindling,
that every moment be full of the screaming sky,
    that the world be a storm of screams,
and I wouldn't hear the silence coming over me,
    the car's engine come to a stop.

trans. Theo Dorgan

AN BÁS

Bhí an bás lem ais,
D'aontaíos dul
Gan mhoill gan ghol,
Bhíos am fhéinmheas
Le hionadh:
A dúrtsa
'Agus b'shin mise
Go hiomlán,
Mhuise slán
Leat, a dhuine.'

Ag féachaint siar dom anois
Ar an dtráth
Go dtáinig an bás
Chugham fé dheithneas,
Is go mb'éigean
Domsa géilleadh,
Measaim go dtuigim
Lúcháir béithe
Ag súil le céile,
Cé ná fuilim baineann.

DEATH

Death alongside me,
I agreed to go,
no crying, no delaying,
just appraising myself,
surprised,
saying:
'And so that was
all I was.
Goodbye, then,
mister.'

Now looking back
to the time
death hustled
up for me,
and I had to
give in,
I think I can gather,
even though I'm a man,
the joy of a woman
waiting on her lover.

trans. Mary O'Donoghue

OILITHREACHT FÁM ANAM

Do labhair an tír mar theampall,
Bhí siúl na habhann boimpéiseach,
Do chrom go glúin na gleannta,
Bhí fíor na croise ar ghéaga.

Mar sheanabhean dheabhóideach
Ag déanamh Turas na Croise
Sheas asailín ómósach
Gan aird aige ar dhuine.

Le soiscéal gaoithe d'éisteas,
Bhí naofacht ar an dtalamh,
Anseo do mhair mo chéadshearc,
Níor ghabhas an treo le fada.

D'aiséirigh 'na taisléine,
Is solas ar a leacain,
Is do thionlaic mé go gléineach
Ar oilithreacht fám anam.

Chonac saol mar scéal fiannaíochta
Fadó, fadó, ar maidin,
A mhúnlaigh an tslat draíochta
A bhíonn 'na láimh ag leanbh.

Bhí cailleach chríon sa chúinne,
A dhá hordóig ag casadh

MY SOUL'S PILGRIMAGE

The country spoke like a temple,
a river shuffled on past,
valleys were bent to their knees,
the sign of the cross upon the branches.

    Like a pious old woman
    making the Stations of the Cross
    a reverent little donkey stood
    paying heed to no-one.

The gospel was carried on the wind,
and there was holiness on the earth.
This was where my first love lived.
I hadn't passed this way in a while.

    A vision arose wrapped in a shroud
    with a brightness from her cheeks,
    and she escorted me vividly
    on the pilgrimage of my soul.

I saw life like a tale from the Fianna,
long long ago in the morning,
the way a magic sword takes shape
in the hand of a young boy.

    There was an old shrivelled shrew
    turning both her thumbs

Go tionscalach mar thuirne,
Ag piseogaíocht go gasta.

Iar n-éisteacht lena glórtha
Ba chomharsa an clúracán dom,
Ba chlúracán gach comharsa
Is drúcht na hóige ar bhánta.

Ach thuirling eolas buile
A scoilt an mhaidin álainn
'Na fireann is 'na baineann,
Is chuir ruaig ar chlúracána.

Mar ghadhar ag déanamh caca
Ar fud an tí istoíche,
Nó mar sheilmide ag taisteal
Do bhréan an fios mo smaointe.

Do samhlaíodh dom gur shloigeas
Mórstoirm oíche gaoithe,
B'é deamhan na drúise 'chloiseas
Á iomlasc féin im intinn.

Do chuala an deamhan trím chodladh
Ag satailt ar mo smaointe,
Is do sháigh isteach a chosa
Im fhéitheacha mar bhríste.

tirelessly like a spinning wheel
while she quickly recited spells.

After listening to her piseogs,
those cluricaunes became my neighbours
until every neighbour was a cluricaune
and the mist of youth on the meadows.

But an insane knowledge descended
to divide the beautiful morning,
into male and female,
and chased the cluricaunes away.

Like a dog taking a shit
all over the house in the night,
or like a snail trailing along,
knowledge fouled my thoughts.

I imagined that I had swallowed
a great storm on a windy night
with the demon of lust I heard
rolling around in my head.

I heard the demon in my sleep,
trampling through my thoughts,
thrusting both his feet
into my veins like trousers.

Chonac frog tráthnóna i dtobar
Is deamhan á chur ag léimnigh,
Do chuala deamhan ag cogar
I lár scigireachta béithe.

Bhreithníos an saol go huamhnach
'Bhain saol na gclúracán díom,
Bhí deamhan ag cách á iompar
Mar chruit ar chruiteachána.

Bhí ceol na ndeamhan á sheinm
I solas chíoch na mban,
Ghaibh nóin chun suain ar buile
Is d'éirigh lá ina ghealt.

'Ná taiscigh do chuid fola,'
Do liúigh na deamhain le chéile
'Do fuairis í le dortadh
Ar iasacht ó na déithe.'

Do labhair an taise taobh liom,
Bhí solas ar a leacain,
Bhí neamhinscneacht 'na bréithre
Mar bhíonn i méaraibh leanbh—

'Scoir ded chaoi is éist go fóill,
Ná múch do chroí,
Do tharla Críost ar fhear fadó
Is deamhan á chloí.

Next I saw a frog down a well,
with a demon sending it jumping,
and I heard a demon whisper
amongst some tittering women.

I believed the world was dreadful
that took my cluricaune world away,
for everyone carried a demon
like a hump on a hunchback.

The music of the demons played
in the light of women's breasts.
Noon went angrily to bed
as the day arose like a loon.

'Don't reserve your blood,'
shouted the demons together.
'You received it to pour freely
on loan from the Gods.'

Then spoke the vision at my side,
with a brightness from her cheeks,
and an innocence in her words
as in the hands of a child:

'Halt your ways and listen awhile,
don't suppress your spirit.
Christ happened upon a man long ago,
who was possessed by a demon.

'D'aibíodh Mac Dé a chaint 'na chroí,
Dob fhile é,
Do ghortaigh focal aibidh Chríost
An deamhan go hae.

'Deamhan a rá, sin deamhan a chloí,
Ní fuirist é
An deamhan a rá le fuil do chroí,
Gach uile bhraon.

'Atá an deamhan anois ad chloí,
Ach abair é
I bhfocail d'fhás i ngort do chroí
Is do thaistil féith.

'Is fanfaidh aingeal óg id chroí
Ag iompar ceoil,
Is chífir aingeal i ngach gnaoi
Go deo na ndeor.'

Le soiscéal gaoithe d'éisteas,
Bhí naofacht ar an dtalamh,
Anseo do thug mo chéadshearc
Stracfhéachaint dom ar m'anam.

'The Son of God's words ripened
in his heart for He was a poet,
and those wise words of Christ
injured the demon to his very being.

'To express a demon is to slay a demon.
It isn't easy
to express a demon with your full heart
and every drop of your blood.

'Even now a demon is defeating you,
but express it in words
grown in the field of your soul
and out through your vein,

'and a young angel will dwell in your heart,
playing sweet music,
and you will see an angel in every thing
for now and evermore.'

I listened to the wind's gospel
and there was holiness on the earth.
This was the place where my first love
gave me a glimpse of my soul.

trans. Denise Blake (with Frank Sewell)

CEOL

Do dhún an ceol an t-aer,
　　Do chrap an spás máguaird,
Bhí fallaí ceoil gach taobh,
　　Is fuaimdhíon os mo chionn.

Bhí leabhar filíochta agam
　　Istigh im cheolphríosún,
Filíocht ón mBreatain Bhig
　　Nár fháiltigh romham ar dtúis:

Mar do bhrúigh mionchaint an tsaoil
　　Thar dhroim gach smaoinimh chugham,
Ach do theasc an ceol an saol
　　De radio mo chluas.

Bhí ualach ceoil am bhrú,
　　Bhí leabhar filíochta fúm,
Do rugas barróg dhlúth
　　Ar véarsa beag banúil,

Is do phógas beol ar bheol
　　An beol ón mBreatain Bhig
Is bhí ceol ag brú ar cheol
　　Is ceol trí cheol ag cith.

SONG

Song closed up the air,
    space contracted all about,
walls of song on every side,
    a roof of sound above.

I had a book of poetry
    within my music-prison,
poetry from Wales
    that would not let me in at first:

for worthless chatter
    swarmed into all I thought,
but song switched off the worldly talk
    within the wireless of my ear.

A burden of song weighed on me,
    I had a book of poetry nearby,
and took in my embrace
    a little feminine rhyme,

and mouth to mouth I kissed
    that mouth from Wales,
and music swarmed on music,
    music raining into music.

Le fód dem intinn féin,
　　Is fód ón mBreatain Bhig
Do chruiceogas an t-aer,
　　Dhein both sa cheol istigh.

With a sod of my mind
    and a sod from Wales,
I'll make a turf-stack of the air,
    a beehive cell within the song.

trans. Ciaran Carson

OILEÁN AGUS OILEÁN EILE

I: Roimh dhul ar oileán Bharra Naofa

Tá Sasanach ag iascaireacht sa loch,
Tá an fhírinne rólom ar an oileán,
Ach raghad i measc na gcuimhne agus na gcloch,
Is nífead le mórurraim mo dhá láimh.

Raghad anonn is éistfead san oileán,
Éistfead seal le smaointe smeara naomh
A thiomnaigh Barra Naofa don oileán,
Éistfead leo in inchinn an aeir.

II: Amhras iar ndul ar an oileán

A Bharra, is aoibhinn liom aoibhneas do thí
Agus caraimse áitreabh do smaointe,
Ach ní feas dom an uaitse na smaointe airím
Mar tá daoscar ar iostas im intinn.

Le bréithre gan bhrí,
Le bodhaire na mblian,
Thuirling clúmh liath
Ar mo smaointe.

Mar chloich a cúnlaíodh
Do hadhlacadh iad,
Do truailleadh a gclaíomh
Im intinn.

THIS ISLAND AND THE OTHER ISLAND

I. Before going to Saint Finbarr's island

An Englishman is fishing in the lake,
over on the island the stark truth rests.
I will go among the rocks and memories
and bathe my hands with reverence.

I will go across and listen to the island,
listen to the essence of saints' thoughts
bequeathed by St. Finbarr to the island,
listen to them in the mind of the air.

II. Doubts before stepping on the island

Finbarr, your joyous home delights,
this genial place of reflection,
but are these thoughts sourced from
or the rabble dwelling in my mind?

From words without fervour
and the deafness of my years,
there is a mossy mould
growing over my thoughts.

Like a rock layered in lichen
my thoughts have been buried,
the sharp sword of my mind
has long been corrupted.

Naoimh is leanaí
A bhogann clúmh liath
De cheannaithe Chríost
Nó de smaointe.

Tá an t-aer mar mhéanfuíoch
Ar m'anam 'na luí,
Bhfuil Barra sa ghaoith
Am líonadh?

Tá Barra is na naoimh
Na cianta sa chria
Is dalladh púicín
Ad bhíogadh.

Tá tuirse im chroí
Den bhfocal gan draíocht,
Bíodh dalladh nó diabhal
Am shiabhradh.

III: An bíogadh

Tá ráflaí naomh san aer máguaird
Is an ghaoth ag fuáil tríd,
Tá paidir sheanda im chuimhne i léig,
Is mo smaointe á séideadh arís.

Anseo ar bhuaile smaointe naomh
Do léim chugham samhail nua,

Only children and saints
can loosen the damp moss
from the features of Christ
or from thoughts.

The air is like a yawn
on my sleeping soul.
Is Finbarr in the breeze
restoring me?

But Finbarr and the saints
are long cast under clay,
so confusion must deceive me
like a trickster.

My heart is weary
of words without mystery.
Dazzlement or some devil
holds me under a spell.

III. The rousing

The air is full with whispers of saints
as the wind threads on through;
in the back of my memory an old prayer,
and my thoughts are stirred up once more.

Here in this place of holy thoughts
a new image leapt out at me;

Do chuala tarcaisne don saol
I nguth an éin bhí 'clagar ceoil.

An ceol a raid sé leis an mbith
Dob shin oileán an éin,
Níl éinne beo nach bhfuair oileán,
Is trua a chás má thréig.

IV: Oileán gach éinne

I bhfírinne na haigne
Tá oileán séin,
Is tusa tá ar marthain ann
Is triall fád dhéin,
Ná bíodh ort aon chritheagla
Id láthair féin,
Cé go loiscfidh sé id bheatha tú,
Do thusa féin,
Mar níl ionat ach eascaine
A dúirt an saol,
Níl ionat ach cabaireacht
Ó bhéal go béal:
Cé gur cumadh tú id phaidir gheal
Ar bhéal Mhic Dé
Do scoiltis-se do thusa ceart
Le dúil sa tsaol,
Ach is paidir fós an tusa sin
Ar oileán séin,
A fhan go ciúin ag cogarnach

I heard contempt for our chosen world
in the sound of a bird's clacking chorus.

The song he shared with the universe
was the bird's own island.
No-one is born without an island—
a pity for anyone who deserts.

IV. Each one's island

There's an island of serenity
in the mind's truth.
It is you who resides there,
so go to meet your self.
Don't tremble with fear
in your own presence,
although your self
will burn you alive,
as you're just a curse
uttered by the world,
just some loose talk
from mouth to mouth:
though formed as a prayer
on the mouth of our Lord,
you cleaved from the right you
to craven life,
but the right you
is still a prayer
on an island of serenity,

Ar bheolaibh Dé
Nuair do rincis-se go macnasach
Ar ghob an tsaoil.

V: Oileán Bharra Naofa

Tráthnóna ceathach sa Ghuagán,
Ceo ag creimeadh faille,
Do chuardaíos comhartha ar oileán,
Do fuaireas é i gcrannaibh.

Im thimpeall d'eascair crainn chasfháis,
Dob achrannach a leagan
Do lúbadar 'ngach uile aird
Mar chorp á dhó ina bheatha.

Mar scríbhinn breacaithe ar phár
Is scríbhinn eile trasna air
Chonac geanc is glún is cruit is spág,
Fá dheoidh chonac dealramh Gandhi.

A Bharra, chím i lúib na ngéag
Gur troideadh comhrac aonair
Idir thusa Dé is tusa an tsaoil
Anseo id gheanclainn naofa.

Nuair ghlanann ceo na feola léi
Tig áilleacht ait i rocaibh,

and stayed whispering softly
on the lips of God
while you went romping
on the gob of the world.

V. St. Finbarr's island

A showery afternoon in Gougane Barra
as a full fog gnawed at the cliffs,
I searched the island for some sign
and found it there within the forest.

Twisted trees appeared around me,
all misshapen and entangled,
writhing outwards in every direction
like a body being burned alive.

I saw, like writing on a piece of parchment
with more writing across and over it,
a snub nose, a knee, a hump, a clumsy foot
and, finally, I saw the likeness of Gandhi.

Finbarr, I see in the bend of the branches
how you fought your own deadly duel
between God's you and the world's you,
here in this holy place of snub noses.

When the fog of the flesh disappears
it leaves the strange beauty of scars,

Is féidir cló a mheas ann féin
Sa tsolas cnámhach folamh.

Tá sult na saoirse i gcló na gcrann
Is grá don tsúil a fiaradh,
Tá dúil sa rud tá casta cam
Is gráin don bhog is don díreach.

Is fireann scríbhinn seo na gcrann,
Níl cíoch ná cuar in aon bhall,
Tá manach scríte abhus is thall,
Sé Barra lúb na ngéag seo.

A insint féin ar Fhlaitheas Dé,
Ag sin oileán gach éinne,
An Críost atá ina fhuil ag scéith
An casadh tá ina bhréithre.

Is macasamhail dá oileán féin
Oileán seo Bharra Naofa,
An Críost a bhí ina fhuil ag scéith
An phúcaíocht ait i ngéagaibh.

VI: An Sasanach agus mé féin

Tá Sasanach ag iascaireacht sa loch
Is measaimse gur beag leis an t-oileán,
Ach ní feasach dom nach iascaireacht ar loch
Don Sasanach bheith ionraic ar oileán.

true forms will be judged for themselves
in the empty skeletal light.

Freedom joys in the script of the trees
and here love warps the eye,
there's passion for things jagged and crooked,
abhorrence for the smooth and untried.

This tree-script is masculine,
there's not a breast or curve in sight.
Monk is written everywhere,
and this tangle of limbs is Finbarr.

Every individual's island
is their own version of Heaven,
and the Christ who flows in their blood
is the twist and turn in their words.

This blessed place of St Finbarr
is the replica of his own island,
with the Christ who flowed in his blood
spookily disguised in branches.

VI. The Englishman and myself

An Englishman is fishing in the lake with
scant regard for this island,
but I believe that fishing in this lake
may still give rise to his personal island.

Raghad anonn is fágfad an t-oileán,
Fágfad slán le smaointe smeara naomh,
Raghad ag ceilt na fírinne mar chách,
Raghad anonn ag cabaireacht sa tsaol.

I will go now and leave this island,
bid farewell to the saints' sacred thoughts.
Burying the truth like others before me,
I will rejoin the babble of this world.

trans. Denise Blake (with Frank Sewell)

NA BLASCAODAÍ

(dán nár críochnaíodh)

Ólaidh deoch im fhochairse,
A Fheara an oileáin,
Tá uaigneas na mara oraibh
Is uaigneas na mbád,
Níl aon chéile leapa agaibh
Ná leanbh i gcliabhán,
Ach do thugabhair libh an aigne
Chomh húr le leanbhán
A thréigeamar i leabharaibh
Is pairilis ina cnámha,
Is a fhanann linn sa duanaire
Mar a fhanabhair ar oileán
Go dtí go dtagann fonn orainn
Suirí le seanadhán.

Ólaidh deoch im fhochairse,
A Fheara an oileáin,
Tá uaigneas na mara oraibh
Is uaigneas na mbád,
Tá uaigneas na leabhar oraibh
Is uaigneas na ndán,
Is fá thuairim ár seanaigne
Déanam ólachán.

THE BLASKETS

(unfinished)

Come drink with me,
you island men,
with your sea-strangeness
and boat-strangeness,
you've no partner in bed
or child in the cradle
but bring with you
the mind as fresh
as a new-born babe,
which we left paralysed
in pent-up tomes,
but which waits for us
in our book of songs
like you did on an island
till the notion took us
to indulge in old poems.
Come drink with me,
you island men
with your sea-strangeness,
and boat-strangeness,
your strangeness still
of verse and book,
I raise a glass
to our old outlook.

■

Do thaisteal naomhóga san aer,
Bhí an Blascaod Mór imithe le gaoith,
Do shín Inis Tuaisceart sa spéir
Mar dhealbh shaighdiúra i gcill,
Mar Thaibhse le teampall a éag
Bhí an Tiaracht ag fanacht le Dia.

Níl iontu ach cuimhne ár sean
Ar snámh ins an aer os ár gcionn,
An chuimhne fho-intinneach lean
Ag fo-chogarnach ionainn go ciúin
Is striapachas intinn' 'nár measc
Is eachtrannacht focal máguaird.

Agus d'fhan sí sa ghrinneall mar ghrean
Gur múchadh na focail máguaird,
Is bhí an file gan solas gan dath
Go dtáinig sí chuige ar cuairt,
Ball seirce i bhfocal do las,
Is d'imigh go grinneall athuair.

A dhuine atá ag spealadh an fhéir,
Cad ab áil leatsa ar uachtar talún?
Níl ionat ach cuimhne ó chéin,
Ag baint fhéir sa tsamhlaíocht taoi, monuar,
Is an t-asal ag inbhear led thaobh,
Asal fo-intinneach súd!

■

Currachs were rowing upon the air,
the Great Blasket gone with the wind,
Inishtooskert stretched out in the sky
like a soldier's statue in a graveyard,
and Tearaght, like the Scripture of a church
that died, was waiting there for God.

They're only our elders' memory
floating above us in the air,
the subconscious memory continuing
to sound in low whispers within
while promiscuous thought divides us
and alien words close round.

Like sand on a seabed, the memory waited
for those words to quieten down,
the poet without light and colour
till it came to him on a visit,
set alight a tryst of words
and sank back down to the seabed.

And you who are mowing grass,
what do you seek on the surface?
You're only a far-flung memory,
making hay in the imagination
with an ass grazing beside you,
that braying ass—the subconscious!

Tá tigín fo-intinneach bán
Ag machnamh ar imeall Dhún Chaoin
Inar chuala caint chianda mná
Is í dall ins an leaba le haois,
Is do chonac an fho-intinn ar barr,
Is an bharrintinn deascaithe thíos.

Bhí aigne Pheig mar naomhóig
Ár n-iompar ar dhromchla na dtonn,
Chuaigh ár gcúrintinn éadrom go tóin
Nocht ár bhfo-intinn folaigh mar chúr,
Ghaibh imigéiniúlacht ár nglór,
Bhí mianach macalla sa bhfuaim.

Níor chualamar riamh an macalla
Ach ag filleadh ó chnocaibh i gcéin,
Ach anseo tá an stáisiún forleatha
Óna gcraolann an macalla féin,
Tá imigéiniúlacht 'nár n-aice,
Is aisiompú eagair san aer.

Deep in thought at the edge of Dún Chaoin
is a white house in the subconscious
where I listened to the ancient speech
of a bed-ridden woman, blind with age,
and saw on the surface the deeper mind,
shallow reason dumped to the bottom.

Peig Sayers's brain was like a currach
that carried us across the waves,
sinking the froth of our foam-thoughts,
and raising the deep mind from the foam
until a strangeness came over our speech,
and an echo rang in the sound.

We'd only ever heard the echo
come back faintly from far-off hills,
but here's the broadcasting station
from which the echo is transmitted,
the long distant within our reach,
and power shifting in the air.

trans. Frank Sewell

SAOIRSE

Raghaidh mé síos i measc na ndaoine
De shiúl mo chos,
Is raghaidh mé síos anocht.

Raghaidh mé síos ag lorg daoirse
Ón mbinibshaoirse
Tá ag liú anseo:

Is ceanglód an chonairt smaointe
Tá ag drannadh im thimpeall
San uaigneas:

Is loirgeod an teampall rialta
Bhíonn lán de dhaoine
Ag am fé leith:

Is loirgeod comhluadar daoine
Nár chleacht riamh saoirse,
Ná uaigneas:

Is éistfead leis na scillingsmaointe,
A malartaítear
Mar airgead:

Is bhéarfad gean mo chroí do dhaoine
Nár samhlaíodh riamh leo
Ach macsmaointe.

LIBERTY

I will go down amongst the people
on foot
and I will go down tonight.

I will go down seeking bondage
from the venom liberty
that howls here:

and I will tie the pack of thoughts
that snarl around me
in the solitude:

And I will seek an ordered temple
where people congregate
at a set time:

And I will seek out people
who never practised liberty
or solitude:

And I will listen to the shilling thoughts
that are exchanged
like money:

And I will give the love of my heart to people
who never imagined
other than second hand.

Ó fanfad libh de ló is d'oíche,
Is beidh mé íseal,
Is beidh me dílis
D'bhur snabsmaointe.

Mar do chuala iad ag fás im intinn,
Ag fás gan chuimse,
Gan mheasarthacht.

Is do thugas gean mo chroí go fíochmhar
Don rud tá srianta,
Do gach macrud:

Don smacht, don reacht, don teampall daoineach,
Don bhfocal bocht coitianta,
Don am fé leith:

Don ab, don chlog, don seirbhíseach,
Don chomparáid fhaitíosach,
Don bheaguchtach:

Don luch, don tomhas, don dreancaid bhídeach,
Don chaibidil, don líne,
Don aibítir:

Don mhórgacht imeachta is tíochta,
Don chearrbhachas istoíche,
Don bheannachtain:

Oh, I will remain with you day and night,
And I will be lowly
And I will be faithful
to your stub-thoughts.

Because I heard them grow in my mind,
grow without control,
without moderation.

And I gave them my heart's love fiercely
to the thing that is bridled,
to every copied thing:

To discipline, to law, to the peopled temple,
To the poor and commonplace word,
to the set time:

To the abbot, the bell, the servant,
to the hesitant comparison,
to cowardice:

To the mouse, to measurement, to the tiny flea,
to the chapter and the line
of the alphabet:

To the majesty of going and coming,
to gambling at night,
to salutations:

Don bhfeirmeoir ag tomhas na gaoithe
Sa bhfómhar is é ag cuimhneamh
Ar pháirc eornan:

Don chomhthuiscint, don chomh-sheanchuimhne,
Do chomhiompar comhdhaoine,
Don chomh-mhacrud.

Is bheirim fuath anois is choíche
Do imeachtaí na saoirse,
Don neamhspleáchas.

Is atuirseach an intinn
A thit in iomar doimhin na saoirse,
Ní mhaireann cnoc dar chruthaigh Dia ann,
Ach cnoic theibí, sainchnoic shamhlaíochta,
Is bíonn gach cnoc díobh lán de mhianta
Ag dreapadóireacht gan chomhlíonadh,
Níl teora leis an saoirse
Ná le cnoca na samhlaíochta,
Ná níl teora leis na mianta,
Ná faoiseamh
Le fáil.

To the farmer measuring the wind
in the autumn as he thinks
of a field of barley:

To co-understanding, to co-tradition
to co-behaviour of co-people,
to the co-copied thing.

And I bestow my hatred now and forever
on the doings of liberty
on independence

Weary is the mind
that has fallen in the deep trough of liberty,
no hill erected by God exists there,
only abstract hills, the particular hills of the imagination,
and each hill is full of desires
climbing, unfulfilled,
liberty is without limit,
so are the hills of the imagination
the desires are unlimited,
and there exists
no release.

trans. Seán Ó Ríordáin

IFREANN

Cé go bhfacasa adharca
Chomh cumtha le teampall,
Is óigbhean ag iompar
Banúlachta seanda,
Is suaimhneas na gaibhneachta
Ar mhiotala sleamhaine,
Tá mo smaointe chomh coillte
Le déad fiacal mantach.

Tá fairsingeacht smaointe
San abairt is lú,
Tá síneadh don intinn
I mbeag is i mór,
Tá iascaireacht machnaimh
Sa tsolas máguaird,
Ach tá m'anamsa i gcarcair,
I bpeaca beag duairc.

HELL

Although I have seen horns
as shapely as a temple,
and a young woman bearing
ancient womanliness,
and the serenity of smithy work
on smooth metals,
my thoughts are as ruined
as the ivory of a chipped tooth.

There's breadth of thought
in the smallest sentence,
and stretching of mind
in what's great or small,
there's fishing for thought
in the light all around
but my soul's imprisoned
in the gloom of venial sin.

trans. Theo Dorgan

SIOLLABADH

Bhí banaltra in otharlann
I ngile an tráthnóna,
Is cuisleanna i leapachaibh
Ag preabarnaigh go tomhaiste,
Do sheas sí os gach leaba
Agus d'fhan sí seal ag comhaireamh
Is do bhreac sí síos an mheadaracht
Bhí ag siollabadh ina meoraibh,
Is do shiollaib sí go rithimeach
Fé dheireadh as an seomra,
Is d'fhág 'na diaidh mar chlaisceadal
Na cuisleanna ag comhaireamh:
Ansin do leath an tAngelus
Im-shiollabchrith ar bheolaibh,
Ach do tháinig éag ar Amenibh
Mar chogarnach sa tseomra:
Do leanadh leis an gcantaireacht
I mainistir na feola,
Na cuisleanna mar mhanachaibh
Ag siollabadh na nónta.

SYLLABICATION

A nurse in a hospital
on a sunlit afternoon,
and pulses in sick-beds
beating to her measure,
she stood above each patient
in studied concentration,
jotting down the rhythm
that beat between her fingers,
then left the pulses beating,
and beat it from the room,
leaving behind a chorus
of pulses beating on:
then the Angelus sounded
on syllable-shaken lips
till round the room it faded
to a dying Amen;
but the chanting continued
in the abbey of the flesh,
the pulses like monks
reciting the syllables
of afternoon prayer.

trans. Seán Ó Coileáin, Seán Ó Mórdha,
Frank Sewell, Robert Welch

DÁN

blúire de dhán fada

Ní loirgím aon véarsa
Ach an véarsa d'fhás go ciúin
Gan timireacht ó éinne,
Chomh dúchasach le glúin,
Chomh héasca i gcrot le glúin.

Mar thoircheas i mbroinn
Bíodh an véarsa seo a chím,
Ní iarraim ach a iompar
Idir an dá linn,

Ná ní mian liom a cheistiú
Mura seoltar chugham a bhrí,
Mar ní liomsa féin a bhrú,
Ná ní liomsa féin a bhrí.

Bhí lámh ag mo sheanathair ann,
Cé nár chleacht sé riamh filíocht,
Ach bhí duanaire bó bainne aige
Sa bhfeirm i gCiarraí.

Is do thuig sé cad ba chrú,
Is do thuig sé cad ba chíoch,
Is do bheirimse mo bhuíochas dó
Gur chuimil sé siní.

A POEM

an excerpt from a long poem

I seek no verse
but a verse that grew silently,
with no one in attendance,
as natural as any generation,
as nimble in shape as a knee.

Let this verse that I see be
in the womb like a pregnancy;
all I ask is to carry it
in the interim,

nor do I wish to interrogate it
if its meaning isn't delivered to me
because it's not my womb gestates it;
I am not the one who gives it vigour.

My grandfather had a hand in it,
though he never practiced poetry,
he had a milch-cow anthology
on his farm in Kerry.

And he knew about milking,
and he understood the pap,
and I give him thanks
that he stroked the teats.

Do bhlais a lámh an tsine sin,
Is do thuig a brú ó chroí,
Cneas le cneas do tuigeadh é,
Mar fhear ag luí le mnaoi.

Do fágadh bainne i bhfocalaibh,
An fhírinne i gcích,
Ní neamhionann crú na bhfocal san
Is sniogadh na siní.

His hand tasted that teat,
his heart knew how to press it,
skin to skin he felt it,
like a man and woman together.

Milk infused in words,
in the pap the truth,
milking those words is not unlike
draining those teats dry.

trans. Colm Breathnach

from Brosna (1964)

A GHAEILGE IM PHEANNSA

A Ghaeilge im pheannsa,
Do shinsear ar chaillis?
An teanga bhocht thabhartha
Gan sloinne tú, a theanga?

Bhfuil aoinne inár dteannta
Ag triall ar an tobar?
Bhfuil aon fhocal seanda
Ag cur lenár gcogar?

An mbraitheann tú pianta,
Dhá chíoch bhfuilid agat?
Pé cuma ina luífeá,
Arbh aoibhinn an t-amharc?

Pé cluas ar a luífeá
San oíche, pé eagar
Ina dtítfeadh do chuail dheas cnámhsa, a theanga,
'mBeadh fhios ag an easpag, an bráthair, an sagart
Nár chuí dóibh aon mhachnamh rómhór ar do bhallaibh,
Ar eagla an pheaca?

An leatsa na briathra
Nuair a dheinimse peaca?
Nuair is rúnmhar mo chroíse
An tusa a thostann?

TO THE IRISH IN MY PEN

O Irish in my pen
have you lost your ancestors?
Are you a poor fosterling
without any surname?

Is there anyone amongst us
drawing from the well?
Is there any old wise saying
to give volume to our whispering?

Do you feel pain?
Have you full breasts?
Whatever way you lie
would it be a lovely sight?

Whatever ear you rest on
in the night, whatever shape
your fine bundle of bones might take, O language,
would the bishop, brother, priest know
not to look too long
on your limbs
for fear of sin?

Are the words yours
when I commit sin?
When my heart is secretive
are you the one silences it?

An suathadh so i m'intinn,
An mbraitheann tú a shamhail?

Do d'iompar atáimse,
Do mhalairt im chluasaibh,
Ag súrac atáirse
Ón striapach allúrach,
Is sínim chughat smaointe
A ghoideas-sa uaithi,
Do dhealramhsa a chímse,
    Is do mhalairt im shúilibh.

Do you suffer the same
confusion as me?

I am carrying you,
your opposite in my ears,
sucking as you are
on that foreign trollop
while I slip you thoughts
that I've stolen from her.
I see your true image,
     and your opposite in my eyes.

trans. Noel Monahan

RIAN NA GCOS

Anois ba mhaith liom bualadh leis
    Nuair nach féidir é,
Ó dheas a ghabh sé an mhaidin sin,
    Aneas ní thiocfaidh sé.

Maidin ghréine i gCiarraí,
    Ba chlos trithí sruthán
Mar ghlór cailín fé cheilt sa chlaí
    Is mé ag dul thar bráid.

Do shiúil sé liom an mhaidin sin,
    Ár mbeirt ar aon chosán,
Ag siúl ar ais sea tuigeadh dom,
    Chonac rian a chos sa láib.

Ní raibh sé ann gur imigh sé,
    Ní hann go has go brách,
An duine sin 'tá imithe
    Atá sé siúd iomlán.

Mo dhuine bocht 'bhí i bhfara liom,
    Go raibh a anam slán,
Is anam gach a leanfaidh é
    Dem dhaoinese go brách.

Is liomsa anois na cosa sin
    Ar shiúil sé leo sa láib,

THE FOOTPRINTS

I would encounter him one more time
    now that it can't be done.
Southwards he headed that morning,
    never again to return.

A morning of sun in the kingdom of Kerry
    and through it the stream
like a girl's soft voice from a nearby ditch,
    and me lost in a dream.

He walked alongside me that morning,
    two of us on the one road,
but coming home brought it home to me—
    his footprint in the mud.

He wasn't quite there until he was gone,
    not there till gone forever,
that other one who is altogether gone
    and is himself now altogether.

My poor companion, my travelling friend,
    I bid his soul *slán*,
and the souls of all who'll follow his path,
    each one of me, my clan.

They are mine now, those self-same feet
    that carried him

Ach ní mé a bhí i bhfara leis
    Ag éisteacht le sruthán.

Níor saolaíodh mé gur cailleadh é,
    Is mó mé i mise amháin,
Cailltear le gach focal mé,
    Ach éiríonn le gach anáil,

An mé nua sin a leanann mé
    Go gcomhlíontar mise amháin;
Scata a scrí' na ranna seo,
    Duine as gach anáil.

Sceo ar sceo do scumhadh iad,
    Na daoine seo dem chroí,
Ní hionadh gurb ionmhain liom rian
    A gcos sa láib im shlí.

through the mud; but it wasn't me beside him
    listening to a stream.

I never was born till he was dead—
    there's many a me in myself,
one lost with every word uttered
    rising with every breath

the new me now who walks in my wake
    till one entire me is complete;
a host of selves scribbled these verses,
    one born each time I breathe.

Strip by strip they were peeled away,
    these folk of my heart, my blood.
No wonder that I cherish their footprints
    on my way through the mud.

trans. Francis O'Hare

CLAUSTROPHOBIA

In aice an fhíona
Tá coinneal is sceon,
Tá dealbh mo Thiarna
D'réir dealraimh gan chomhacht,
Tá a dtiocfaidh den oíche
Mar shluaite sa chlós,
Tá rialtas na hoíche
Lasmuigh den bhfuinneoig;
Má mhúchann mo choinneal
Ar ball de m'ainneoin
Léimfidh an oíche
Isteach im scamhóig,
Sárófar m'intinn
Is ceapfar dom sceon,
Déanfar díom oíche,
Bead im dhoircheacht bheo:
    Ach má mhaireann mo choinneal
    Aon oíche amháin
    Bead im phoblacht solais
    Go dtiocfaidh an lá.

CLAUSTROPHOBIA

Beside the wine
is a candle. And fear.
Our Lord's statue
has lost all its power.
What the night holds
is a horde in the alley.
Outside my window,
night's dark ministry.
If my candle goes out
in spite of my praying,
the night will leap up
and into my lung,
the fear will invade,
and take over my mind
till I'm living night,
darkness defined;

      but if my candle holds out
      through this one night,
      until the day comes
      I'll be a republic of light.

trans. Francis O'Hare

AN FEAIRÍN

*Ní Ezra Pound atá i gceist anseo, ach duine de na cainteoirí
dúchais Gaeilge is binne agus is oilte sa tír. Ní fear beag é ach an
oiread ach taibhsítear don té a chíonn é go bhfuil gach ball dá
bhaill beag toisc go bhfuil cuma na huaisleachta ar a phearsa.*

'Theastódh tigh is gort ón bhfeairín bocht,'
A dúirt an bhean 'dtaobh Pound,
Is bhailigh Pound isteach sa bhfocal di
Is chónaigh ann.

Ní fhaca Pound iomlán go ndúirt sí é,
Is do scrúdaíos é ó bhonn
Fé ghnéithe an teidil sin a bhaist sí air,
Is dar liom gur dheas a rogha.

Tá beirthe ar Phound sa bhfocal sin aici,
Mar feairín is ea Pound,
Do réitigh gach a bhfuil dá chabhail sa bheatha léi,
Ó bharr a chinn go bonn.

Tá buanaíocht age Pound sa bhfocal sin,
Tá suaimhneas aige ann,
Is pé duine eile 'bheidh míshocair inár n'aigne,
Ní mar sin a bheidh Pound.

THE MANEEN

Not Ezra Pound, but one of the best and most educated Irish
speakers in the country. Nor is he a small man but he gives the
impression of compactness because he has the appearance of
nobility.

He'd need a house and land,
the maneen, said the woman about Pound,
and Pound crept into the word
and settled there.

I didn't see Pound fully until she said it,
and as I looked him up and down
in the light of her christening,
it seemed a fine choice.

Pound has been reborn in that word of hers
because Pound *is* a maneen;
from the top of his head right to the ground,
the whole of his body agrees with her.

Pound is fixed in that word,
he has peace there,
and whoever else is uneasy in our minds,
it won't be Pound.

trans. Peter Sirr

GUÍ

Iarraim ar an naofacht imeacht uaim,
Más í a chím,
Is eagal liom tréigean datha,
Is eagal liom brí,
Is bás, dar liom fós, freagairt,
Is beatha fiafraí,
Ragham amú tamall eile,
Is chífeam an tír.

Iarraim filíocht bheag a cheapadh
Anois is arís,
Ní iarraim go ndéanfainn peaca,
Ba bhaoth mo ghuí,
Ná go gcuirfeadh neach eile a anam
I mbaol an dlí:
Dá mbeimis ó bhaol an pheaca
Dob fhearr filíocht.

Ach iarraim go mbraithfinn tarrac
An tsaoil im chroí,
Iarraim go bhfeicfinn trí Phól is a theagasc
An Pól atá thíos
Ag gliúcaíocht aníos tríd an Laidin
Is cealg ina chroí:
Ós amhlaidh atá, ós amhlaidh ár ngairm,
Is amhlaidh mo ghuí.

A PRAYER

I ask sanctity to leave me
if that's what I'm seeing;
I fear the colour growing weak
and I am afraid of meaning.
To answer is death, to my mind,
to be alive is to inquire;
let us go astray yet a while
and take in the countryside.

I ask that I should compose
some little poems now and again;
I don't ask that I should sin
—that prayer would be in vain—
nor that another would put his soul
in danger of conviction:
if we were free of sin's peril
poetry would be better then.

But I ask that I'd feel the appeal
of the world in my heart,
and that I'd see through Paul and his teaching
to the Paul under it, standing apart
peering slyly from beneath the Latin
with guile in his heart:
    as things are thus, as our calling is such,
    that is what I ask.

trans. Colm Breathnach

REO

Maidin sheaca ghabhas amach
Is bhí seál póca romham ar sceach,
Rugas air le cur im phóca
Ach sciorr sé uaim mar bhí sé reoite:
Ní héadach beo a léim óm ghlaic
Ach rud fuair bás aréir ar sceach:
Is siúd ag taighde mé fé m'intinn
Go bhfuaireas macasamhail an ní seo—
    Lá dar phógas bean dem mhuintir
    Is í ina cónra reoite, sínte.

STIFF

One frosty morning as I ventured out
a handkerchief on a bush seemed to carry such clout
I seized on it and tried to pay
it into my pocket but, being frozen, it slipped away.
This was no living remnant torn
from my grasp but something that expired last night on a
        thorn.
I cast about for a likeness till something fetched
up from deep within
      my memory—that day I kissed one of my own kith and kin
      who was stiff as a board in her coffin, stiff and stretched.

trans. Paul Muldoon

NA LEAMHAIN

Fuaim ag leamhan leochaileach, iompó leathanaigh,
Bascadh mionsciathán,
Oíche fhómhair i seomra na leapa, tá
Rud leochaileach á chrá.

Oíche eile i dtaibhreamh bhraitheas-sa
Peidhre leamhan-sciathán,
Mar sciatháin aingil iad le fairsingeacht
Is bhíodar leochaileach mar mhná.

Dob é mo chúram lámh a leagadh orthu
Is gan ligean leo chun fáin,
Ach iad a shealbhú gan sárú tearmainn
Is iad a thabhairt chun aoibhnis iomlán.

Ach dhoirteas-sa an púdar beannaithe
'Bhí spréite ar gach sciathán,
Is tuigeadh dom go rabhas gan uimhreacha,
Gan uimhreacha na fearúlachta go brách.

Is shiúil na deich n-uimhreacha as an mearbhall
Is ba mhó ná riamh a n-údarás,
Is ba chlos ciníocha ag plé le huimhreacha,
Is cách ba chlos ach mise amháin.

THE MOTHS

Moth-tender sound, a page being turned,
    wounding of tiny wings,
autumn night, all through the bedroom,
    a soft thing suffering.

Another night, in a dream, I felt
    a moth's gentle wingspan.
Overarching, angelic, but infinitely
    bruiseable, like woman.

I had to lay my hands on them
    and not let them flutter away,
and deliver them to bliss,
    and not violate their sanctuary.

But me, I spilled the magic powder
    sprinkled on each wing,
and knew I'd always lack the numbers,
    the numbers of the masculine.

The ten numbers strode from the chaos,
    greater than ever in authority,
and nations were heard engaging in numbers,
    and all were heard but me.

Fuaim ag leamhan leochaileach, iompó leathanaigh,
Creachadh leamhan-scannán,
Oíche fhómhair is na leamhain ag eiteallaigh
Mór mo bheann ar a mion-rírá.

Moth-tender sound, a page being turned,
    moth-membrane in ruin,
autumn night, full of moth-fluttering,
    their tiny ructions my great concern.

trans. Francis O'Hare and Frank Sewell

SEANMÓINTÍ

Sagart ag scréachaigh gach Domhnach,
Glór i gcóitín ins an teampall,
Seanmóintí iad gan amhras,
Fothram focal le clos.

Caithfidh a shamhail bheith ann leis,
Ó tharla sé caithfidh sé labhairt linn,
Fuair sé a ionad sa teampall,
I lár an phobail istigh.

Pé acu searbh nó binn linn a chlampar
Bhí sé le bheith ann d'réir dealraimh,
Ceapadh ó thosach an domhain dó
Go mbeadh a thamall aige.

Cé nach ceolmhaire é ná an gandal,
Cé nár mheasa linn éisteacht le srann muc,
Is binne ná téada ag labhairt é,
Mar tá cláirseach an Mháistir aige.

HOMILIES

Sunday after Sunday, the turned-up
petticoated screech of the priest in church.
Homilies, yes, that much is certain:
noise, audible words.

The like of him must also exist;
since there he is, speak he must.
He has found his niche inside the church,
surrounded by the congregation.

Sweet or sour, whatever we make of him,
he was, by all accounts, to be.
It was laid out from the very beginning
that he, also, would have his hour.

Yes, he has less music than a gander's cackle,
and to listen to a pig couldn't be harder;
yet his speech is even sweeter than strings,
because the Master's harp is his.

trans. Paddy Bushe

A THEANGA SEO LEATH-LIOM

Cé cheangail ceangal eadrainn,
A theanga seo leath-liom?
Muran lán-liom tú cén tairbhe
Bheith easnamhach id bhun?

Tá teanga eile in aice leat
Is deir sí linn 'Bí liom,'
Do ráinig dúinn bheith eadraibh,
Is is deighilte sinn ó shin.

Ní mór dúinn dul in aice leat
Go sloigfí sinn ionat
Nó goidfear uainn do thearmann,
Is goidfear uaitse sinn.

Ní mheileann riamh leath-aigne,
Caithfeam dul ionat;
Cé nach bog féd chuid a bhraithim tú,
A theanga seo leath-liom.

LANGUAGE HALF-MINE

Who tied this knot between us,
dear language half-mine?
What's the use in handling you
unless you are all-mine?

There's another tongue beside you
and she says to me. 'Be mine,'
Caught between the two of you,
we're separated since then.

Now I must get close to you
till I'm fully absorbed,
or I'll be robbed of your refuge
and you'll be robbed of me.

Half a mind to do won't do,
I have to fully enter in,
though you're a hard one to get round,
language half-mine.

trans. Mary O'Malley and Frank Sewell

FIABHRAS

Tá sléibhte na leapa mós ard,
Tá breoiteacht 'na brothall 'na lár,
Is fada an t-aistear urlár,
    Is na mílte is na mílte i gcéin
    Tá suí agus seasamh sa saol.

Atáimid i gceantar bráillín,
Ar éigean más cuimhin linn cathaoir,
    Ach bhí tráth sar ba mhachaire sinn,
    In aimsir choisíochta fadó,
    Go mbímis chomh hard le fuinneog.

Tá pictiúir ar an bhfalla ag at,
Tá an fráma imithe ina lacht,
Ceal creidimh ní féidir é bhac,
    Tá nithe ag druidim fém dhéin,
    Is braithim ag titim an saol.

Tá ceantar ag taisteal ón spéir,
Tá comharsanacht suite ar mo mhéar,
Dob fhuirist dom breith ar shéipéal,
    Tá ba ar an mbóthar ó thuaidh,
    Is níl ba na síoraíochta chomh ciúin.

FEVER

The bed-hills are ever so high,
fever the humidity in their midst,
the floor a long, long way off,
    and miles and miles away
    are sitting and standing in this world.

We are in sheet-country now
and can hardly remember a chair,
    but before we became a meadow,
    way back in our walking time,
    we stood as high as a window.

A picture on the wall is swelling,
the frame has melted into liquid,
with faith absent, this can't be stopped;
    things are closing in on me,
    and I can feel the world collapse.

A district is shooting from the sky,
a neighbourhood poised on my finger,
I could easily grasp a chapel;
    on the road north there are cows,
    and cows in eternity are not as still.

trans. Frank Sewell

DAOIRSE

Dá labhródh bean leat íseal
Ná hísleofá do ghuth?
Dá mbeadh an bhean réasúnta
Ná réasúnófaí tú?
Ach gheobhair san ísleacht uaisleacht
Mar uaisleofar do ghuth,
Is tabharfar sa réasúntacht
Míréasúnú duit:
Dá mhéad a ghéillfir uaitse
Is ea is lú éileofar ort,
Ná tabhair don daoirse diúltamh
Is tabharfar saoirse duit,
Mar domhan is ea an tsaoirse,
Is tír gach daoirse inti,
Is níl laistigh d'aon daoirse
Ach saoirse ón daoirse sin.

LIMITATION

If a woman spoke to you in a low voice
wouldn't you lower your own?
And if the woman reasoned with you,
wouldn't you be made to reason?
But you'll find nobility in humility
as your voice will be ennobled.
And in the reasoning
you'll be given unreason:
the more you submit
the less will be demanded of you.
Don't baulk at limits,
and you'll be given freedom.
Because freedom is a world,
and every limit a country within it.
And all that's in any limitation
is freedom from its limits.

trans. Celia de Fréine

TOST

Is fada mise amuigh,
Is fada mé im thost,
Is nach fios nach amhlaidh bheidh go deireadh scríbe;
Ní cuimhin liom go baileach,
Dá mhéad a mhachnaím air,
Cár leagas uaim an eochair oíche ghaoithe:
Tá m'aigne fé ghlas,
Níl agam cead isteach
Le go ríordánóinn an farasbarr neamhscríte,
Gach barra taoide ait
Dár chraol an mhuir isteach
Ó bhíos-sa féin go deireanach i m'intinn.
Ná bain le dul isteach,
Tá an eochair in áit mhaith,
B'é gur folamh bheadh do thearmann beag iata;
Cuir as do cheann ar fad
An fharraige is a slad,
Is bí sásta leis an aigne neamhscríte.

SILENCE

I'm a long time out of it,
I'm a long time silent,
and who knows but I'll be like that right to the end;
I don't rightly remember,
no matter how often I think of it,
where did I leave the key one windy night;
my mind is locked up,
I have no right of entry
that I might Riordanise the unwritten surplus
brought in on the high tide
and broadcast by the sea
since I was last in my right mind.
Never mind gaining entry,
the key's in a good place
though your little refuge is empty and closed up;
put out of your mind entirely
the sea and its plunder,
be satisfied with the unrecorded mind.

trans. Theo Dorgan

TULYAR

A Tulyar, a Stail
A cheannaigh De Valéra ón Aga Khan,
Tír mhór geanmnaíochta tír mo shean,
Tír maighdean, tír ab,
Tír saltar is soiscéal,
Is bráithre bochta ar mhórán léinn,
A Tulyar, sin stair:
Ach cogar, a Stail,
Nach dóigh leat é bheith ait
Ceardaí ded cheird, ded chlú, ded chleacht,
Ded chumas breise thar gach each,
A theacht
Ag cleachtadh a cheirde anseo inár measc
I dtír na n-ollamh, tír na naomh,
An tír a bheannaigh Pádraig féin?
Ní hé gur peaca cumasc each,
Ach suathadh síl ab ea do theacht;
Ní soiscéal Phádraig thugais leat
Ach intinn eile
'Thuigfeadh Eisirt;
Is lú de pheaca peaca, a Stail,
Tú bheith i mbun taithí inár measc,
Id stail phoiblí, lán-oifigiúil,
Thar ceann an rialtais ag feidhmiú.

TULYAR

Ah, Tulyar, auld stallion,
De Valera's prize-buy from the Aga Khan,
it's a pure-living land my ancestral land,
a land of comely maidens, a land of priests,

a land of psalm-books and Gospels
and poor holy Brothers rich in knowledge.
Tulyar, *a mhic*, that's ancient history.
But c'mere, auld stallion, listen:

does it not sit somehow at all strange with you
that an artist of such craft and distinction,
not to mention your unequalled technique,
should be coming over here

to practice his magic among us
in the land of scholars and saints,
the land blessed by Patrick himself?
Not that I'm damning all horseplay

but it's a quare turnaround, your coming,
and it's not Patrick's gospel you're preaching
but another way of thinking entirely,
one more mindful of Eisirt;

An é go rabhamar fachta seasc,
Gur theastaigh sampla stail' inár measc?
Nó an rabhamar dulta eiriciúil
Mura ndéanfaí tusa oifigiúil?

and there's no sin in sinning now, auld horse,
with you swinging your thing here among us,
a public stud, with official endorsement,
conducting affairs on behalf of the government.

Was it that we were found wanting
that a real stallion was brought in among us?
Or would it be deemed uncanonical
if you hadn't been given state sanction?

trans. Francis O'Hare

AN LACHA

Maith is eol dúinn scéal na lachan,
Éan nár gealladh riamh di
Leabhaireacht coisíochta:
Dúchas di bheith tuisleach
Is gluaiseacht léi ainspianta
Anonn is anall gan rithim,
Is í ag marcaíocht ar a proimpe:
Ba dhóigh leat ar a misneach
Gur seo chughat an dán díreach
Nuair is léir do lucht na tuigse
Gur dícheall di vers libre.

THE DUCK'S TALE

is well known:
a bird unblessed
with litheness of limb,
by nature a staggerer,
awkwardly moving
to and fro
without any rhythm,
and riding so high
upon her tailbone
that you would take her
for perfect metre
when those in the know
know, at best
she's *vers libre*.

trans. Frank Sewell

COLM

Do Cholm, mac Shéamais Uí Mhurchú, dealbhóir

Buanghol, a Choilm, do cheol,
    Ach oireann an deor do d'aois,
Taoi bliain ar an saol anocht,
    Is do thugais le gol trí mhí

A Choilm cheansa, fáth do bhróin
    Lig liomsa, d'athair baistí;
Do laghad féin, an é is cúis leis,
    Do mhionsamhail féin nuair ná facaís?

Cé taoi mion, a mhic go fóill,
    Fairsingeoir le himeacht blian,
Ní hionann is an dream docht
    A chum d'athair as cloch is cria.

Ní náir duit bheith mion go fóill,
    Ní féidir roimh am fearú,
Bíonn cion ar an mion i dtoirt,
    Don mion i meon is gnáth fuath.

COLM

for Colm, son of Seamus Murphy, sculptor

Eternal crying is your music, Colm,
    but at your age tears are no surprise.
You're a year in the world tonight
    and you've wept at least three months of that.

Little Colm, let me, your godfather,
    find out the cause of your sorrow;
maybe it's that you're small and can't see
    anyone else who looks like you.

But for all that you're small just now,
    the years will soon see you grow
unlike the stiff crew
    your father made from stone and clay.

There's no shame in being small,
    you can't be a man before your time;
for smallness of form there's affection,
    but smallness of mind no-one will abide.

trans. Peter Sirr

CATCHOLLÚ

Is breá leis an gcat a corp,
Is aoibhinn léi é shearradh,
Nuair a shearr sí í féin anocht
Do tharla cait 'na gceathaibh.

Téann sí ó chat go cat
Á ndúiseacht as a ballaibh,
Fé mar nár chat í ach roth
De chait ag teacht is ag imeacht.

Í féin atá sí ag rá,
Is doirteann sí slua arb ea í
Nuair a shearrann an t-iomlán,
Á comhaireamh féin le gaisce.

Tá na fichidí catchollú
Feicthe agamsa anocht,
Ach ní fichidí ach milliúin
'Tá le searradh fós as a corp.

INCATATION

The cat worships her body,
just loves to unravel;
when she shook herself tonight,
it rained cats by the catful.

She turns from cat into cat
at the stir of a paw;
more like a wheel than a cat,
shifting to and fro.

She expresses herself,
sheds a catalogue of skins;
at full-stretch, she counts
herself and preens.

Tonight I've seen scores
of incatations;
and still to come,
not scores but millions.

trans. Frank Sewell

FILL ARÍS

Fág Gleann na nGealt thoir,
Is a bhfuil d'aois seo ár dTiarna i d'fhuil,
Dún d'intinn ar ar tharla
Ó buaileadh Cath Chionn tSáile,
Is ón uair go bhfuil an t-ualach trom
Is an bóthar fada, bain ded mheabhair
Srathar shibhialtacht an Bhéarla,
Shelley, Keats is Shakespeare:
Fill arís ar do chuid,
Nigh d'intinn is nigh
Do theanga a chuaigh ceangailte i gcomhréiribh
'Bhí bunoscionn le d'éirim:
Dein d'fhaoistin is dein
Síocháin led ghiniúin féinig
Is led thigh-se féin is ná tréig iad,
Ní dual do neach a thigh ná a threabh a thréigean.
Téir faobhar na faille siar tráthnóna gréine go Corca
            Dhuibhne,
Is chífir thiar ag bun na spéire ag ráthaíocht ann
An Uimhir Dhé, is an Modh Foshuiteach,
Is an tuiseal gairmeach ar bhéalaibh daoine:
      Sin é do dhoras,
      Dún Chaoin fé sholas an tráthnóna,
      Buail is osclófar
      D'intinn féin is do chló ceart.

RETURN AGAIN

Leave the Valley of the Mad back east,
and all there is of this age of our Lord in your blood,
close your mind to what has happened
since the Battle of Kinsale,
and, since the load is heavy
and the road long, remove from your mind
the civilised halter of English,
Shelley, Keats and Shakespeare:
return again to your own,
cleanse your mind and cleanse
your tongue which got tied up in a syntax
at odds with your intellect:
make your confession and make
peace with your own race
and with your own house, and do not abandon them.
It is not natural for anyone to abandon his house or his tribe.
On a sunlit evening take the cliff road out to Corca
        Dhuibhne,
and out on the horizon you will see shoaling there
the Dual Number, and the Subjunctive Mood,
and the vocative case on people's mouths:
    that is your door,
    Dún Chaoin in the evening light,
    knock and there will be opened
    your own mind and your right shape.

trans. Barry McCrea

from Línte Liombó *(1971)*

LÍNTE LIOMBÓ

Mo ghreidhin iad na línte
A chaitheas a dhiúltú
Nuair phreabadar chun tosaigh
Le bheith ina gcuid de dhán:
Tá a malairt anois ceapaithe
In oifig go postúil,
Is gan ionad don dream diúltaithe
Im chruinnese go bráth.
Cá bhfios dom nárbh iadsan
Dob fhearr a dhéanfadh cúis,
Dob fhearr a chuirfeadh mise
Ins an rud a bhí le rá?
Ach ambasadóirí eile
A sheolas uaim chun siúil,
Fé mar ná beadh ina malairt
Ach aicme gan aird.
Dá nglacfaí leis na línte sin
Dob éigean a dhiúltú,
Cén mise nó frithmhise
A chífí im scathán?

LIMBO LINES

I'm bemused by the lines
that I had to turn down
when they dashed forward
to be part of a poem.
Substitutes have now
been officially installed
with no place in my world
for the rejected crowd.
But how do I know that they
weren't the better words,
for putting my *self*
into what had to be said,
better than the ambassadors
I appointed in their stead
as though any alternative
would be a useless lot?
Had I accepted the lines
that I had to turn down,
which me or *alter*-me
would I see in the mirror?

trans. Celia de Fréine

SÚILE DONNA

Is léi na súile donna so
A chím i bplaosc a mic,
Ba theangmháil le háilleacht é,
A súile a thuirlingt ort;

Ba theangmháil phribhléideach é,
Lena meabhair is lena corp,
Is míle bliain ba ghearr leat é,
Is iad ag féachaint ort.

Na súile sin gurbh ise iad,
Is ait liom iad aige,
Is náir liom aghaidh a thabhairt uirthi,
Ó tharla sí i bhfear.

Nuair b'ionann iad is ise dhom,
Is beag a shíleas-sa
Go bhfireannódh na súile sin
A labhradh baineann liom.

Cá bhfaighfí údar mearbhaill
Ba mheasa ná é seo?
An gcaithfeam malairt agallaimh
A chleachtadh leo anois?

Ní hí is túisce a bhreathnaigh leo,
Ach an oiread lena mac,

BROWN EYES

They're hers, the brown eyes
I see in her son's face.
It was a meeting with beauty itself
when they lighted on you.

It was a unique connection, too,
with her mind, with her body.
A thousand years disappeared
when they looked at you.

And because the eyes are hers,
it's strange to see them in him,
and I don't want to face her now
appearing in a man.

When she and they were all to me
I never would have thought
that they would become a man's,
the eyes that expressed a woman.

Could any cause of bewilderment
be found worse than this?
Must I learn another language
to address her eyes in him?

She's not the first who saw with them,
any more than her son,

Ná ní hé an duine deireanach
A chaithfidh iad dar liom.

Ab shin a bhfuil de shíoraíocht ann,
Go maireann smut dár mblas,
Trí bhaineannú is fireannú,
Ón máthair go dtí an mac?

and neither is he the last,
I'd say, who'll make use of them.

Is that all eternity means, then,
a small part of us living on,
through one gender and another,
from the mother to the son?

trans. Mary O'Donoghue

AISTRIÚ

Aistrigh a cló cait
Id aigne go bean,
Agus chífidh tú
Go mba bhreá an bhean í
Dá mbeifeá id chat fireann.

TRANSFER

her cat-form
in your mind
to a woman
and you'll find
a fine figure
of a woman
if you were
a tom.

trans. Frank Sewell

TAR ÉIS DOM É CHUR GO TIGH NA NGADHAR

Ná bí am buaireamh a ghadhair,
Fáilte tú chuireas den saol,
Ba tú an fháilte a bhíodh fial romham,
Cé mé chuir deireadh led ré.

Taoi id aonar anois a ghadhair,
Más gadhar fós tú is nach scáil,
I measc do namhad gan trua duit,
Ag fanacht le goin do bháis.

Bhí do chroí gadhair fial, mór,
Ní raibh de mhaoin agat ach grá,
An dream a ghráis d'fheall ort,
Is gan ionat, monuar, ach gadhar fáin.

Bhí béasa gadhair tí agat,
Is támáilteacht gadhair fháin,
Níl ded ghrá rothaig sa mbith anocht
Ach a bhfuil im chroí ded chrá.

AFTER SENDING HIM TO THE DOGHOUSE

Don't be at me like this, dog.
I had to do it.
You were my warmest welcoming friend,
though it was me that had to end your days.

You're on your own now, hound,
if you're still a dog and not a shade,
surrounded by enemies without mercy
as you wait for the death wound.

Your big dog heart was always loyal,
love was all you had in the world,
but the ones you loved betrayed you,
and you only a poor old stray.

You had the ways of a house dog
with the deference of a stray.
Now all that's left of your bounding love
is here in my sore heart tonight.

trans. Mary O'Malley (with Frank Sewell)

CLÓ

Gach rud dá dtagann,
imíonn is ath-thagann,
is filleann arís ár gcéadghlóire;

is deineann fear aibidh
mar a dhein sé ina leanbh,
níl i ndán ach athnuachan ár n-óige.

Nuair a saolaítear leanbh
níl dul aige thairis,
saolaítear an méid a saolófar.

Imímid as amharc
uainn féin gach re tamall,
ag tnúth lenár malairt inár gcló féin,

ach fillimid folamh
i ndeireadh gach aistir,
is séala síoraí ár gcéad chló orainn.

MOULD

All things that are
depart and re-appear,
there returns our original glory;

the mature man behaves
like he did as a baby,
our childhood renewed is all that's in store.

When a child is born
he has no choice,
all he will be is born and no more.

Every now and again
we disappear from ourselves,
hoping to reappear in a different mould,

but we return empty
at each journey's end
with the eternal seal still shown on us.

trans. Colm Breathnach

SOLAS

Do thit an oíche diaidh ar ndiaidh
Go dtí gur mhúch an uile rud,
Do dhein comhdhubh de dhubh is geal,
Do chaill cathaoireacha a gcruth,
Do chuaigh an seomra ar ceal,
Do shloig an dubh an uile chruth:
I mbroinn na doircheachta tá domhan,
Is féidir liom é bhrath lem láimh,
Níl fanta ach a chuimhne agam,
Is leisc lem chuimhne é athchruthú.

Do lasas solas is de gheit
Do saolaíodh seomra im shúil,
Do phreab cathaoireacha as dubh,
Do las mo mhéaranna ina riocht,
Is do chruthaigh solas domhan.

Do mhúchas solas is do mhúch
Mo dhá láimh is a raibh
Le feiscint roimis sin den mbith.

Nuair a bheidh mo sholas múchta ar fad
Fágfad domhan im dhiaidh 'na riocht,
Ach fágfad é sa doircheacht.

LIGHT

Night fell slowly, slowly
until everything was extinguished,
what had been black or bright one equal dark.
Chairs lost their form,
the room was annulled,
the dark swallowed every shape:
there's a world in the womb of darkness,
I can touch it with my hands.
All that remains to me is its memory,
my mind's reluctant to re-create it.

I lit a lamp, and suddenly
a world sprang to life in my eye,
chairs leaped from the dark,
my fingers flamed in their shape
and light made a world.

I doused the light and I quenched
my two hands and what there was
to be seen until then of existence.

When my light is completely gone out
I will leave behind me the world in its form,
but I will leave it in darkness.

trans. Theo Dorgan

NÍ CEADMHACH NEAMHSHUIM

Níl cuil, níl leamhan, níl beach,
Dar chruthaigh Dia, níl fear,
Nach dualgas dúinn a leas,
Níl bean; ní ceadmhach neamhshuim
A dhéanamh dá n-imní;
Níl gealt i ngleann na ngealt,
Nár chuí dhúinn suí lena ais,
Á thionlacan an fhaid
A iompraíonn thar ár gceann,
Ár dtinneas-ne 'na mheabhair.

Níl áit, níl sruth, níl sceach,
Dá iargúlta iad, níl leac,
Bídís thuaidh, thoir, thiar nó theas,
Nár cheart dúinn machnamh ar a suíomh,
Le gean is le báidhíocht;
Dá fhaid uainn Afraic Theas,
Dá airde í gealach,
Is cuid dínn iad ó cheart:
Níl áit ar fuaid na cruinne
Nach ann a saolaíodh sinne.

AGAINST INDIFFERENCE

There's not a fly nor a moth nor a bee
that God created, not a man
nor a woman made we're not
obliged to aid, whose anxiety
we're allowed to disregard;
no man buried in his asylum
we shouldn't sit beside,
keeping him company as long
as he carries on our behalf
our own sickness in his mind.

There's no place, no stream, no bush
however remote, no stone
north, south, east or west
whose site we shouldn't think of
with sympathy and fondness;
however far South Africa,
however high the moon,
they're part of us by right—
there's nowhere in the world
where we have not been born.

trans. Peter Sirr

DOM CHAIRDE

Cuireann sibh olc orm agus ní gan fáth;
Seasaíonn bhur gcainteanna lánmhara,
bhur dtuairimí údarásacha,
bhur dtacaíocht d'bhur n-aicme bheag,
don éagóir atá ag an láidir á imirt ar an lag
sa domhan so inniu,
agus leis na mílte bliain,
ar scáth an teagasc éithigh,
tá sibhse fós a chraoladh,
thar ceann na fírinne dá gcreidfí sibh,
in ainm Chríost tá coillte agaibh:
troidfead sibh go bás,
cé sibhse mo chairde,
mar cloisim macalla ard
bhur gcainte, fan pasáistí
ar fuaid na staire,
ag déanamh eirligh,
ag satailt.

TO MY FRIENDS

You make me sick, and not without reason:
your smug speeches, your high opinions,
the way you protect your own little coterie,
they represent the unfair play
the powerful pit against the weak
in the world today, and for thousands of years,
under the cover of false intelligence
you still broadcast in the name of truth
or the Christ whom you have castrated.

I will fight you to the death,
even though you are my friends,
because I can hear echoing loudly
throughout the passages of history
your rhetoric shocking and awing.

trans. Frank Sewell

MISE

Sin é,
Sin inspioráid,
Sin mise.
Níl d'inspioráid ar an saol domhsa,
Ach mise,
Ná duitse,
Ach tusa.
Ach cá bhfaighead é,
Sé sin mise?
Níl fail air san áit a mbímse.
Ná ní san áit a mbíonn sé,
Ina aonair,
A bhímse,
mar bímse ar aimsir ag an saol,
Sé sin,
Ag daoine seachas mise.
Fillfead air,
Sé sin ormsa,
Ar leaba ár mbáis.

ME

That is it,
that is inspiration:
me.
There's no inspiration in the world for me
but me.
Nor for you
but you.
But where can I find him—
me, that is?
There's no finding him where I am,
and where he tends to be,
alone,
you won't find me,
because I'm out on hire to the world,
i.e.
to people other than me.
But I'll return to him,
that is, to me,
on our deathbed.

trans. Frank Sewell

from Tar Éis mo Bháis *(1978)*

NUAIR A THÁINIG FEARG ORM LE
MUINTIR NA GAELTACHTA

Trínne séideadh fearg,
Sí machnaimh séideadh trínn,
Bímís lom mar charraig,
Bímís dírithe,
A bhuíon ionmhain fuair géilleadh uainn is gnaoi.

Suífeam seal ag machnamh,
Uille ar ghlúin díomhaoin,
Tuigtear dom gur neartaigh
Grá ár bhfearg libh,
A bhuíon ionmhain fuair géilleadh uainn is gnaoi.

Ragham uaibh bóthar fada
Soir ar luas le gaoith,
Fearg sinne ag taisteal,
Ní mhaireann dínn ach í,
A bhuíon ionmhain fuair géilleadh uainn is gnaoi.

Sibhse glór ár n-athar,
Cad dob áil linn díbh?
Cad dob áil linn taca
Seachas teannta ár gcroí,
A bhuíon ionmhain fuair géilleadh uainn is gnaoi?

Sibhse sinne is dearbh,
Is gach ar lean sibh riamh,

WHEN I BECAME ENRAGED WITH GAELTACHT PEOPLE

Rage has blown up between us,
a whirlwind of thought has whistled through us.
Let us be plain as a rock,
let us be straight,
my dear people who received our love and homage.

Let me sit awhile reflecting,
elbow on my knee in vain.
It occurs to me that love
has fuelled our rage at you,
my dear people who received our love and homage.

Let me go far away from you
east with the speed of the wind,
nothing left of us
but rage on the move,
my dear people who received our love and homage.

You are the voice of our fathers.
What did we want of you?
What support did we need
but our own hearts to sustain us,
my dear people who received our love and homage?

We are you, definitely,
as are all who have come after you,

Idir chroí is mheabhair is fhearg,
Is bior bhur n-abairtí,
A dhream ionmhain thug dúinne láthair tí.

Bhur lasair tá in easnamh
Ar lasracha an tsaoil,
Is gile anois bhur lasadh
Bhur múchadh a bheith linn,
A bhuíon ionmhain thug dúinne clocha aoil.

Má mhúchann bladhm bhur lasrach
Lá codlata i nDún Chaoin,
Ní iomlánófar lasracha
Tá easnamhach dar linn,
A bhuíon ionmhain chuir os ár gcionn an díon.

in heart and mind and anger
and the sharpness of your sayings,
my dear people who gave us a site for a house.

Your flame is missing
from the world's fire,
and is all the brighter now
your oblivion is at hand,
my dear people who gave us limestone blocks.

If another flame quenches yours
one sleepy day in Dún Chaoin,
the fire will not be full
but still lacking, according to us,
my dear people who put the roof over our head.

trans. Noel Monahan

GAOTH AN FHOCAIL

Siúd na focail dá bhfiaradh
Fé shéideadh na gaoithe,
Siúd beirthe ag an scríb ar na focail;
Siúd ag insint na gaoithe iad
Is ag iompar a mbríonna,
Siúd dúbailte oifig na bhfocal;
Siúd an duine is a shinsear
Ar mhaoilinn na gaoithe,
Dá shéideadh chughainn focal ar fhocal
I dtreo na síoraíochta,
Gan cónaí gan faoiseamh,
Go gcuirfear clabhsúr ar gach cogar.

WORDS ON THE WIND

See how the words bend
under the weight of the wind,
how they are snatched away in a gust:
they narrate the wind now
bearing also their own meanings,
and there's the burden doubled;
there's man and all of his kind
borne on the cusp of the wind
towards us, word after word
to the end without end
without relief or respite
until all whispers are silenced.

trans. Paddy Bushe

DO STRIAPACH

Do chuais led cheird, is bail ó Dhia ort
Nár dhein fé cheilt do ghnó, a striapach,
Is taoi chomh lom anois id intinn,
Chomh mór gan maíomh gan éirí in airde,
Gur geall le naomh tú, a bhean gan náire.

TO A PROSTITUTE

You took up your trade, and God bless
you, prostitute, for not hiding your business,
and now your mind's so bare and blameless,
humble, without haughtiness,
shameless woman, you're near to saintliness.

trans. Mary O'Donoghue

MO BHÁS FÉIN

Tá aithne agam ar mo bhás féin,
Seanaithne;
Braithim go bhfuaireas bás fadó,
An bás céanna a gheobhad ar ball:
Nuair a chuimhním ar mo bhás
Ní ar rud nár tharla a chuimhním
Ach ar rud a tharla fadó,
Rud a chuaigh as mo cheann,
Rud a dearmhadadh.
Nuair a thagann an intinn seo dom
Tuigtear dom gurb é mo bhás
An rud is mó ná mise:
Is mó is mise mo bhás
Ná a gcaithfead dem shaol iomlán.
Fear saibhir is ea mise
Ar chuma an uile dhuine
Mar sé an bás mo chiste;
Ní féidir baint leis áfach,
Ní féidir do bhás a chaitheamh
Go n-aibeoidh sé;
Talamh nach féidir a dhíol
Nó airgead ceangailte síos
Is ea ár mbás i gcaitheamh ár saoil.

MY OWN DEATH

I know my own death, indeed I know it too well;
I feel I died the same death
long ago that I'll die in time to come again.
When I imagine my death,
it's not as something not happened yet
but as a thing that happened in the distant past,
something that slipped my mind, a forgotten fact.
When I get to thinking this way,
I realise my death is greater than me:
I am more my death
than I am all of my life that I'll live.
I am a rich man, as everyone is,
because death is my wealth;
it can't be drawn on, however,
you can't spend your death
until it has matured;
throughout life our death remains
money that's tied down or property we can't sell.

trans. Colm Breathnach

TAR ÉIS MO BHÁIS

Nuair a fhéachas sa scáthán do chonac
Laistiar dem dhrom mo dhá láimh,
Is tuigeadh dom ar dhath a gcnis
Go rabhas á bhfeiscint tar éis mo bháis,
Nár liom a thuilleadh an dá rud
Laistiar dem dhrom—ná rabhas iontu:
Gur mar sin a shamhlódh mo chorp,
Is mé ar deighilt uaidh tar éis mo bháis,
Go bhfanfadh sé ansúd folamh,
Ina chuid den domhan iomlán,
Is mise fós ag eitilt liom,
Neamhspleách ar fhuil, ar fheoil, ar chnámh,
Chím chugham mé féin gan corp umam,
Ach fós mo scáth 'om thionlacan.

AFTER MY DEATH

When I looked in the mirror I could see
my two hands behind my back,
and could tell from their pallor
I was glimpsing them after my death.
I no longer owned the two entities
behind my back. Nor did I inhabit them.
This was how my body would seem
when we had parted after my death.
It would remain there, hollow,
a part of the whole universe,
while I was still afloat, free
of blood, of flesh, and of bone.
I see myself approach, bodiless,
though my shadow follow on.

trans. Celia de Fréine

BANFHILE

Is ait liom bean a bheith ina file,
Tuigtear dom gur gairm staile,
Cúram fireann, dúthracht raide,
Is ea filíocht a bhaint as teanga:

Le fórsa fireann, éigean buile,
Tugtar slán an ghin chun beatha;
Is mó ná ait liom file baineann,
As an mnaoi a baintear leanbh,

Deacair di a bheith ina hathair.
An é go n-iompaíonn baineann fireann
Nuair a iompaíonn bean ina file?
Ní file ach filíocht an bhean.

Ag luí léi féin a bhíonn banfhile,
Trom léi féin a bhíonn banfhile,
Ní file ach filíocht an bhean.
Á coilleadh féin a bhíonn banfhile,

Á líonadh féin a bhíonn banfhile,
Ní file ach filíocht an bhean.
Fireannach baineann nó baineannach fireann—
Deacair a rá ciacu í an banfhile,

SHE-POET

I find women poets strange.
It's stud-hard work, I think,
a man's duty, a devotion granted,
to draw poetry from language.

With male force, fury, violence,
the impulse to art is birthed safely,
so a female poet is unnatural, for me,
because a woman is a child-bearer,

and she can hardly be a father.
Or is there a sex-change involved
when a woman becomes a poet?
A woman's not a poet, but a poem.

The she-poet lays herself,
rough-rides herself, the she-poet.
A woman's not a poet, but a poem.
The she-poet neuters herself,

fertilizes herself, the she-poet.
A woman's a poem, not a poet.
A sissy or tomboy—hard
to tell what she is, the she-poet.

Ní file ach filíocht an bhean.
Má théann na béithe le filíocht
Is gearr go nginfidh siad leanaí
Gan cabhair ón bhfireannach ina mbroinn,

Is ní file ach neamhní an fear.

A woman's not a poet, but a poem.
And if women consort with poetry
they'll soon conceive children
without any call for men.

Then a man's nothing, not even a poet.

trans. Mary O'Donoghue

AN DÁN DÚR

Is beag tuiscint idir daoine
I seomra feithimh an ospidéil—
Gach aigne ag feitheamh le fuascailt
Ón bhfeitheamh uile—sin a bhfuil léir.

Tá tubaist sroichte go dtí daoine,
Dá olcas í is dóigh le cách
Gur measa ainnise na gcomharsan
Ná a chantam féin mí-ádh.

Tá cailín múisiúnta inár measc,
Í ag méanfach drugaithe,
Áilleacht ina haghaidh gan áilleacht,
A corp beag mícheart.

Le laochas nochtann sí a místaid,
Gaisc' dar léi bheith ina díol trua,
Ag sú aird óna bhfuil i láthair,
Ise an t-othar gairmiúil.

Claoine is ea a mustar saonta,
Mo thrua í ina haonar ar ball,
Gan teannta druga ná daoine,
Gan fágtha dá poimp ach leamhas.

Tá Dia freagrach inti,
Táim féin ciontach, freagrach;

THE DOUR POEM

There's scant consideration among those
in the hospital waiting room—
every soul waiting for release
from all the waiting. That much is clear.

Misfortune has been visited on them,
everyone supposing that, no matter how bad
their quota of woe, their neighbours'
misery is worse than their own.

A girl among us, drugged, agape,
slips in and out of sleep,
beauty in her face without beauty,
her small body misshapen.

She wears her condition with valour,
the professional patient,
proud to be deserving of pity,
the focus of those present.

Her naive stance an iniquity,
I pity her on her own in a while
without the support of drugs or people,
nothing left of her show but bad taste.

God is responsible for her,
I too am guilty, responsible,

Éagóir uirthi gach blúire sláinte
Fanta im aigne, im chorp.

Éagóir uirthi gach ball dem éadach,
Is a bhfuil de mhaoin saolta agam,
Mar tá sí bocht i gcorp is in éadach,
Is ina héirim martraithe.

Atmasféar cruiteacháin gan chruit,
A corp amh, neambeo,
Músclaíonn dúil is déistean,
Músclóidh trua go deo.

every scrap of health left in my head
and my body, a crime against her.

Every article of my attire and all
my worldly wealth a crime against her
because she is poor in body and attire,
and in her impaired ability.

A sense of a crook-back without a crook,
her body crude, without life,
arouses both desire and disgust,
and will always arouse compassion.

trans. Celia de Fréine

TEIP

Le linn dom feitheamh le dochtúir
I dTigh na nGealt do scríobhas dán dúr.
Faraoir níor áiríodh mé ina measc;
Ní rabhas ceart fós, ní rabhas im ghealt,
Is d'éalaíos abhaile ar mo chéill leamh.

SHORTCOMING

Waiting for a doctor in a home
for the mad, I wrote a dour poem.
Alas, I wasn't numbered among them.
Not quite right yet, not wholly deranged,
I sloped off home, wits dull and plain.

trans. Frank Sewell

JOYCE

Chuireas a thuairisc im aigne—
A raibh de im chuimhne scagaithe—
Tá sé ina chuid díom chomh dearfa
Le soiscéal Chríost nó an aibítir.

Tá a chéimseata sho-aitheanta
Ag eúiclidiú m'aigne—
Ní hé a thuilleadh é chomh fada liom,
Is mise é ó alpas é.

Ag triopallacht a fhriotalú táim treascartha,
An fhoirmiúlacht laideanta,
Ní mé mé le linn dom machnamh air,
Ach é siúd—tá lagú ann.

Do chomhraiceas le focail i bhfarradh leis,
Tá sé 'om thionlacan—an t-aingealdeamhan:
Scigshagart é ag rá scigaifrinn,
In éide scigaifrinn ifrinn.

Eiriceacht an creideamh a theagasc sé.
Mhúin sé na deich scigaitheanta,
Droim ar ais a ghairm scoil',
Is chothaigh claoine chleasaiceach.

Ciotarúnta a rún is a asarlaíocht,
Géill don bhfocal ainglí,

JOYCE

I sent out a search-party to find
what's left of him in my sifted mind,
he who is as much part of myself
as the alphabet and Christ's gospel.

With his trademark geometry
Euclid-izing my brain, he
(if you ask me) is not he but I'm
he since I absorbed him. His fine

phrasing and classical constructions
leave me flagging in destruction.
I'm not I but he when thinking
of him—it feels like I am shrinking.

I've wrangled over words with him
as my companion, the angel-imp:
a mockpriest saying a mockmass
in the mockrobes of the black abyss,

teaching the religion of heresy,
the ten commandments of parody,
his scholarly mission a turned back—
a classic stance he learned to perfect.

A cunning, contrary craft he offered:
'Yield to the angel-wingèd word,

Loirg scéimh i salachar,
Is coisric cac le Rabelais.

Goid gach bob as leabharaibh,
Aimsigh feall fuaraigeanta,
Bí id Shátan Beannaithe,
Is coinnealbháigh an farasbarr.

Ba mhó de chleas ná pearsa é,
Foclóir bhain geit as gramadach,
Samhlaíocht a mhair ar neamhshamhlaíocht,
Fuair seilbh ar scigabdaine.

look for beauty in the filthy,
bless, like Rabelais, the shitty,

steal every trick in the book,
target the calculating crook
and, like a beatific Satan,
fire out excommunication . . . '

More a trickster than a person,
a wordsmith making grammar bound,
a seer who preyed on dearth of vision,
he was mockheir to a mockmission.

trans. Frank Sewell

ÚDAR

Is é dúirt an t-údar so
Ná scríobhfadh focal go
mBeadh Gaeilge ar a thoil aige.

Do chaith sé a óige mhoch,
Is meán a aoise amach,
Is deireadh a laethanta,
Ag tóraíocht Gaolainne.

Ansan fuair bás de gheit,
Díreach is í aige.

EXPERT

An author once declared
he wouldn't write a word
until he had mastered
Irish.

He threw his whole youth,
middle years and old age
into red hot pursuit
of the language.

Next thing, he died—
just as he qualified.

trans. Frank Sewell

PRÉACHÁN

Tá mná na haoise seo
Níos féile féna gcuid
Ná bantracht óige an fhir:
Trua cás an fhireannaigh
A chaill a chumas fir
Sara mbog an bhaineannach.

CROW

Women of this age
are freer with what they've got
than when the man was in his element.
Pity the male who was past it
before the female sex
relaxed.

trans. Eilish Martin

EIREABLÚ

Fuair sí í féin ina cat,
Dar léi siúd nárbh ait,
Mar bhí sí riamh ina cat—
Ceathairchosach, ciúin,
Eireaball as a tóin,
Radharc san oíche, scrabhadh,
Gomh lapa is mí-amha,
Is í chomh soghluaiste leis an abhainn.

Dá n-iompóinn féin im chat,
Dar liom go mothóinn ait,
Go mba dheacair dom an scrabhadh,
An t-eireaball is an mí-amha,
Do lánshamhlú lem shamhail.

Ní bhraithim ait mo lámh,
Táim inti iomlán,
Ní coimhthíoch liom mo thóin,
Tá sí de réir mo mheoin,
Táim inti intleachtóil,
Ach bheadh ríordánú catbhall
Glan bunoscionn lem mheabhair—
Ba chríocha aineoil im mhapa
Eireaball nó lapa.

TAILED

She found she was a cat.
Nothing strange about that.
She'd always been a cat:
four-footed, quiet,
tail sticking out of her,
supple as a river,
night-sight, scratching, miaows,
and a sting in her paws.

Hard to imagine that,
but if I were to turn cat,
I think I'd find it odd,
the scratching awkward,
the tail, miaow-miaows,
not to mention the claws.

What's not odd is my hand.
It's part of all I am.
And my bum's no stranger.
It goes with my brain here,
making me a full-
fledged intellectual.
But to be cat-suited
tom-tailed, whiskered, booted,
is way beyond my ken.
Off the map for me, man.

Ní bheadh in eireaball ach éadach
Mura bhfásfadh sé díscréideach,
Ag gabháil tionlacain led éirim,
Ribe ar ribe 'od athrú,
Go n-eireablófaí tú catbhuan.

But if a tail were to grow
on you, discreetly, like clothes
and fit you to a tee,
strand by strand you'd be
completely taken over,
top to tail, furever.

trans. Frank Sewell

AN GAD IS GIORRA DON SCORNACH

Chím an duine romham amach
Agus pian mhór air, chím a bhás:

Ach is fuirist dom é féin agus a phian agus a bhás
A chur ar an méir fhada;
Mura gcuirfinn
Ní mhairfinn;
Is leor liom pian an té
Atá faram i láthair na huaire:

Cé gur mise an duine romham amach,
Ní hé mé go fóill,
Agus is cuma liom cén íde a thabharfar air
Nuair ná caithfidh mise an lae inniu
Í fhulang:

Cé go n-aithníonn an fhuil a chéile
Ní trua liom mo mhise féinig—
Achar ó bhaile:

Tá gach mise tá caite dearmhadta, mílítheach,
Is iad súd tá le teacht, tá gach mise acu coimhthíoch:

Ní beag do gach mise
A chuid oilc féin.

THE NOOSE NEAREST THE NECK

I see the person in front of me
his suffering, his death:

so easy for me to ignore him,
his suffering, his death;
for if I do not
I will not survive.
I know well the pain of the man
with me right now:

and though I am the man in front of me,
he is not yet me.
I am not upset by his adversity,
since the man I am today
does not endure his misery.

Even if blood knows its own clan,
I have no pity for my other self
so near to hand.

Every spent me is forgotten, pallid,
every me to come a stranger.

Every single me has enough
hardship of his own.

trans. Denise Blake

CLÓNNA ÜBER ALLES

Tá na clónna ag gabháil thart ar mire,
Cló na con, cló an duine,
Chonac anois beag sceitse de choin,
Ar chlúdach Mheasgra Dánta a hAon,
A deineadh tríocha bliain ó shin.

Tá an chú san sa tsíoraíocht anois,
Ach dá olcas tá an sceitse sin fuinte,
Tá na comharthaí sóirt fé leith a dheineann
Cú de ghadhar soiléir le feiscint:
Tá coin á síolbhú fós inniu,
Agus an cló san con orthu chomh tiubh.

Mar an gcéanna leis an duine,
Tá a shainchló féin air lán chomh socair
Is bhí ar a mhacasamhail sa phortach,
Dhá mhíle bliain tar éis a churtha.

An mar seo tá an scéal mar sin—
Imeom ar nós an tsneachta anuraidh,
Ach fanfaidh na clónna fós ag filleadh,
Leis an bpointeáltacht chéanna cruinnis,
Ag iompar con is duine,
Ár macasamhail, ní sinne?

CLONES *ÜBER ALLES?*

Forms are running all around like wild—
houndform, humanform. Just now I spied
on the cover of Measgra Dánta a hAon
a thirty-year-old sketch of a bounding hound.
By now, that hound is in eternity
but no matter how rough the sketch may be,
it still distinctly bears the marks that set
a hound and dog apart. You can't miss it.
Hounds bred today are as thickly enclosed
in houndform now as in the days of old.
The same goes for every man and woman,
as secure in the one-off form upon them
as our doppelgänger dug from the bog
two thousand years since he went under the sod.
So, is this the way the story goes—
we all fade away like last year's snow
but the forms keep coming back on the scene
with the same pinpoint accuracy,
delivering up a hound or a human
like us but not the same man or woman?

trans. Frank Sewell

SEÁN Ó RÍORDÁIN, A BRIEF CHRONOLOGY

- Born 3rd December 1916, year of the Irish Revolution (Easter Rising). He is the first of three children born to Seán Ó Ríordáin, a cobbler and native Irish speaker, and Mairéad Lenahan who knew no Irish prior to her marriage and little afterwards. He is brought up in the Breac-Ghaeltacht (semi-Gaeltacht or bilingual area) of Ballyvourney, County Cork.
- 3rd March 1926, his father dies from tuberculosis (TB).
- He attends St Michael's National School (Sliabh Riabhach, Ballyvourney) where he is taught by Tadhg Ó Duinnín whom Ó Ríordáin later describes as a 'poet, drinker and teacher.'
- In 1932, when he is fifteen, the young Ó Ríordáin and his family move from Gaeltacht to Galltacht, i.e. to an English speaking area, Inis Cara, near to Cork City.
- 1937, Ó Ríordáin begins work as a clerical officer in the motor taxation office in Cork City Hall.
- 1938, diagnosed with tuberculosis, he is forced to take leave from work and to endure his first long stay (for months at a time) at a TB sanatorium.
- 1943, Ó Ríordáin wins his first Oireachtas award for poetry.
- 1944, several of his poems are published in the March edition of the Irish-language literary journal *Comhar*.
- 21st March 1945, his mother dies and within six months he writes 'Adhlacadh mo mháthar'/'My mother's burial', his 'first great poem' and 'the most important poem in Modern Irish' according to contemporary poet Louis de Paor.
- 1950 sees the publication of *Nuabhéarsaíocht: 1939–1949*. Edited

by Seán Ó Tuama, this landmark anthology draws critical atten-
tion to a new generation of pioneering Irish-language poets led by
Máirtín Ó Direáin, Máire Mhac an tSaoi and Seán Ó Ríordáin.

- 1952, Ó Ríordáin's first collection, *Eireaball Spideoige*, is pub-
  lished. A larger than usual poetry collection, this is a compen-
  dium of the poet's work up to that time. In hindsight, it could
  have been distilled into perhaps two more thematically homoge-
  nous collections. The influence of Gerard Manley Hopkins is
  signalled in the Preface and is seized upon (negatively) by some
  critics who are suspicious of deviations from Irish as it is spoken
  by native speakers. The longer poems are praised for their ambi-
  tion and seriousness, although the influence of T. S. Eliot (also
  cited in Ó Ríordáin's introduction) is less noted.

- 1954, he is awarded Duais an Chraoibhín (a major book prize in
  Irish, dating back to 1936 and named after Douglas Hyde).

- 1964, *Brosna*, a much slimmer collection, is published a full
  twelve years after the publication and mixed reception of his first
  collection. 'The praise can be more damaging than the criticism,'
  Ó Ríordáin typically observed. The main theme of *Brosna* is the
  Irish language itself, although the volume also includes some of
  the poet's best known lyrics on topics such as illness: 'Claus-
  trophobia' and 'Fiabhras'/'Fever.' The collection displays signs
  (linguistic and topographical) of the poet's immersion in the
  Kerry Gaeltacht: 'Fill arís'/'Return again.'

- 1965, Ó Ríordáin's takes early retirement from his clerical post.

- 1967, *Rí na nUile* (King of All), a collection of translations (into
  modern Irish) of early Irish devotional poetry is published. The
  translations are co-written by Ó Ríordáin and Seán S. Ó Conghaile.

- 1967–75, he writes a weekly column in *The Irish Times*. Hugely
  popular for their irreverence, internationalism and linguistic
  play, Ó Ríordáin's journalistic writings arguably divert his energy
  and attention from poetry. Occasionally, however, some cross-
  fertilization occurs between the two genres.

- 1969, *Seán Ó Ríordáin: Filíocht agus Prós*, an LP recording of selected poems and prose passages is released by Gael-Linn (re-released in 2008). This is one of the recordings that poet Nuala Ní Dhomhnaill later listened to while living in Turkey, and which directly influenced her return to Ireland and to writing poetry in Irish.

- 1969–76, Ó Ríordáin is a part-time lecturer at University College Cork. In this position, he exerts some influence over a coming generation of writers, including the *INNTI* poets (including Michael Davitt, Liam Ó Muirthile and Gabriel Rosenstock) and other writers, including Alan Titley, Robert Welch and John Montague.

- 20th May 1970, RTÉ documentary *Writer in Profile: Seán Ó Ríordáin* is broadcast.

- 1971, *Línte Liombó*, Ó Ríordáin's third volume of original poems, is published, accompanied by illustrations by artist Paul Funge (1944–2011). This slim collection, filled out by the artwork, contains some notable work but gives credence to the view, shared by Ó Ríordáin himself, that he was running out of inspiration, and that his best work was in the past.

- 1976, Ó Ríordáin is awarded an honorary D.Litt by the National University of Ireland.

- 21st February 1977, the poet dies in hospital three weeks after writing his final poem, 'Clónna über alles.'

- 1978, *Tar Éis Mo Bháis* is published posthumously. Divided into two sections, this volume includes miscellaneous poems published in journals, mainly *Scríobh 2*, and also some unpublished poems written over several decades. Both sections include some memorable work that has become central to the poet's oeuvre and to its critical reception.

- 1980, *Scáthán Véarsaí*, a selection of Ó Ríordáin's poems, edited by Cian Ó hÉigeartaigh, is published by Sáirséal agus Dill.

AFTERWORD

Cad is filíocht ann?/What is poetry?
Seán Ó Ríordáin's original introduction
to *Eireaball Spideoige* (1952).
translated by John Dillon[1]

What is poetry? Is it a child's mind? Imagine two people in a
room, a child and his father, while a horse is passing by outside. The
father looks out and says, 'That's X's horse going to the fair.'[2] In this
case he is telling. It seems as though the father loses the horse
because it remains outside of him. Say that the horse is a disease.
The father does not catch the disease. The horse does not enrich the
father's life. But the child—he hears the sound of the horse. He
tastes the sound of the horse for the sake of the sound itself. And he
listens to the sound growing fainter and fainter and eventually dying
away into the silence. And to him the sound seems wonderful and
the silence seems wonderful. And he observes the hind legs of the
horse and is astonished at their authority and antiquity. And the
world fills with horse-wildness and incantatory-trotting. That is
being—being in the guise of something else. And that, it seems to
me, is poetry. The child lives in the guise of the horse. Say that a
child's soul is a mould or structure.[3] I am not able to compare a
person's soul to anything else.[4] The expression or mark of the mould
has to be on everything which comes out of it. *Et protulit terra
herbam virentem, et facientem semen juxta genus suum . . .*[5] That
soul or structure is found in a horse, in a language, and in every
other thing, just as Raissa Maritain writes:

In what deep-down region dwell the identities of speech? How
is a foreign language learned by a child? My own experience
leads me to believe that it is not only by adding one particular
bit of knowledge to another, not simply a question of vocabu-
lary and of memory; [. . .] rather the mind receives communi-
cation of a specific form—a form in which all the ramifications
of language are contained, as the ramifications of an oak tree
are contained in the acorn.[6]

And this is how Stephen MacKenna put it: ' . . . although difficult to
explain, the other thing which is quite effective is the spirit of the
language.'[7] I would like to call this original thing, this ideal thing,
which comes out of the mould, a prayer.

When I say that the child lives in the guise of the horse, this is
what I mean—I think. The child has an inscrutable empathy with
every aspect of the horse: its trotting, its neighing, its mane, and so
he is swallowed up, just as Turnbull was swallowed, in the atmo-
sphere of the horse (see the poem 'Malairt'). But while the child
approaches the horse, he does so as a child, not as a horse. Out of his
solitude the child tries to be a horse, to say the horse's prayer. The
child is lonely because he was never a horse, as we are all lonely
when we consider empathetically a path we have not taken. See, for
instance, Eliot's 'Burnt Norton':

Footfalls echo in the memory
Down the passage which we did not take
Towards the door we never opened
Into the rose-garden.[8]

The child is vicariously living the horse-days which he never spent.
But what happens to the structures? In what state are the prayers?
This is a child's effort, a child's prayer. The structure of the child
must be in the attempt. But where did the prayer of the horse
go? Didn't the child attempt to say that prayer? Wasn't the child
immersed in the horse? Didn't the child live in the guise of the

horse? It's unlikely that the child abandoned his own structure. That's something he can't do. But he's not as removed from the horse as the father was—someone who did not taste. If the child were to compose a poem, out of his empathy and his solitude, would the prayer of the horse be in the poem as well as the prayer of the child? I think that they would be if the child succeeded in composing an honest poem (there would also be a third prayer, i.e., the prayer of the poem itself, because it seems as though there is a prayer in every thing—a point to which I'll return). And I'm not talking about mentioning the horse in the poem, nor speaking about a horse. Perhaps a horse wouldn't be mentioned in any way at all, but the spirit of a horse would be felt, just as the spirit of a child and the spirit of poetry would be felt in the poem. For a poem isn't telling but being. Where, then, though, did the prayer of the horse go? I don't think that it is sufficient to say that the prayer of the horse is poured like bronze into the mould of the child.

So how does a person know if he has ever written a line of poetry? How does he know what poetry even is? If the hatred I sometimes have for my poems is an indication of anything, it's that there isn't any poetry in these lines. I've often felt that composing poetry was an unusual task—an activity which isn't writing or shaping, but is closer to cleaning. I'd say that I was like someone who was cleaning rust or mildew off of a statue, searching for and renewing the basic image—searching for bedrock.[9] If we compare this idea of cleaning or digging to the coughing which accompanies a cold, then it is possible to understand the basic image as a lung. Or it is possible to see the activity as a blind man reading Braille.[10] We all recognize the bedrock, this form that was refined from every other form. We don't know how we recognize it, yet we know it to be very old, foundational, authoritative, permanent, and beautiful. And it isn't possible to encounter it without a start[11] of joy. (This is, without a doubt, an ideal description of my own imperfect and dishonest process.)

What is this joyful basic image? Is it our soul, our spirit, our eternal form, our structure? Or is it the structure of that which we contemplate with empathy?

I notice that it is easier to compose a poem on a particular event than on a general subject. It's easier, for example, to compose a poem on a particular death than on death in general. The start comes sooner. And a poem isn't born without a living-start. I think that rubbing creates the start—a friction between our charged aspect and the charged aspect of another thing. But how is it then that a particular death startles us more readily than death as an abstract concept?

I have to begin by explaining my understanding of a prayer. I think that every person, every thing, every flock, every pack of hounds, every family, is able to create a prayer because each has a soul or structure within. They must have a soul because that is the idea from which they spring. And the clay body which we possess is a version of our prayer. It isn't a living version, but a faulty version, a version which is weak, heavy, polluted, and misdirected. It is not urged on by the spirit. It does not tremble eternally with the living-start of the spirit. But after the Day of Judgement we will have a different body which will be perpetually startled. That is the kind of body which Christ had after the Resurrection. And it is the kind of body that Saint Augustine had in mind in chapters XX, XXII, XXIII of the *De Civitate Dei*.[12]

The body which we will have after the resurrection (*that is, if we are saved*) is our perfect prayer, the final statement of our soul. It is a beautiful thing. It has to be beautiful because it is an ideal thing. It is the standard of its own beauty. And compared with it, our clay body is heavy and halt, a Caliban. Nevertheless, while we are living we are able to say a prayer purer than our clay body. We are able to raise ourselves like incense before God by living within an appropriate action. While living, this action is the purest state of our prayer, and I wouldn't be surprised if it were a pre-telling (or a pre-existing, to be more precise) of the body which we will have in eternity. Both of these things will be marked by the seal of our structure, and they will both be startled. This is how Hopkins describes the act:

> As kingfishers catch fire, dragonflies draw flame;
> As tumbled over rim in roundy wells
> Stones ring; like each tucked string tells, each hung bell's
> Bow swung finds tongue to fling out broad its name;
> Each mortal thing does one thing and the same:
> Deals out that being indoors each one dwells;
> Selves—goes itself; myself it speaks and spells,
> Crying *What I do is me: for that I came.*
>
> I say more: the just man justices;
> Keeps grace: that keeps all his goings graces;
> Acts in God's eye what in God's eye he is—
> Christ—for Christ plays in ten thousand places,
> Lovely in limbs, and lovely in eyes not his
> To the Father through the features of men's faces.[13]

But people and prayers are dependent upon each other, and it isn't possible for a person to make a prayer without reflecting upon that which he is not, upon the way he did not go, just as the child did. If a person wishes to raise himself as incense in the presence of God, he finds the incense elsewhere in another person or thing. He has to believe in another form besides his own structure and humble himself to it. He must recognize the external sculpturing of truth and pay homage to it. For a person cannot taste himself. Nor can a person rub against his own self and startle himself. Instead, he startles something other (usually something abstract, such as the act of shoemaking or architecture or nursing). They startle each other. Not only is his own prayer stirred but the prayer of the other thing is stirred as well. The person and the action become active and they co-act or co-pray. Friction occurs between each charged part, between the two acts, the two prayers. Then the start comes, and from the start a new thing, such as a poem or a church or a shoe or a sound, is made which has its own structure and its own prayer. But in this newly made thing there will be the prayers of its progenitors as well as its own prayer. The prayer of the architect, of architecture, and of the church will be found in the church. It follows that abstract things as well as concrete things have a structure, a prayer, and a weak-version. And I believe that that's how it is. And I believe that the weak-version of the architecture is the inactive version.

I know a nurse.[14] Let's say that nursing is her true, characteristic act of prayer, or one of them. One day I met her, and she was an ordinary woman who was not focused on her prayer. It happened, however, that she had to do a task concerned with her profession. At once she became a nurse. I saw the common prayer of nursing—its post-judgement body or shape. I saw nursing in the form of an action. Nursing was praying through her just as she was praying through nursing. The woman in the guise of nursing was the prayer of the woman. The nursing in the guise of the woman was the prayer of nursing. And between them they made something new (the piece of nursing which was done that day) which also had its own prayer. But this woman is part of womankind as well. And so, womankind is often praying through her. She is also a Christian. And she is a dancer. In this respect, there are many things through which a person is praying and many things which are praying through a person. It is appropriate, therefore, to call a person or a thing a temple.

When a person falls into a state of illness or holiness or anger, that state prays at his temple, and there you can hear the pain or the psalm or the fit which is appropriate to his condition.

It appears then that the interaction between prayers is the same as that of life itself or love. And it continues perpetually for it grows out of the desire and solitude which are in us all. People and animals and woods and oranges and arts and every abstract and concrete thing go visiting at each other's temples. I'd imagine that the purity of the abstract thing and the substance of the concrete thing

will be in the post-judgement body, and it is the concrete thing
which covets the purity and the abstract thing which covets the
substance when they encounter each other. And I believe that
horses and woods, languages and seas, will enter eternity with us and
they will be *sub specie aeternitatis*, that is, in the form of perpetual
action, in the form of a prayer. Similar to the post-judgement body
which Saint Augustine discusses, this prayer will have substance as
well as form. And since I think that abstract things will go into
eternity with us, I must give an eternal body and a place in eternity
to things like diseases. Diseases will have post-judgement bodies just
like everything else, but no one will be harmed because by then
prayers will have stopped visiting each other. There will be an end
to praying. An end to uttering. An end to structures. By then the
entire form of truth will be in front of us. But until then, as stated in
Genesis, we will be praying until the coming of the desire of the
eternal woods:[15]

> *Deus patris tui erit adjutor tuus et Omnipotens benedicet tibi
> benedictionibus caeli desuper, benedictionibus abyssi jacentis
> deorsum, benedictionibus uberum et vulvae. Benedictiones pa-
> tris tui confortatae sunt benedictionibus patrum eius, donec ven-
> iret desiderium collium aeternorum.*[16]

Sometimes structures are fused together until they become a
compound prayer, so that multiple things have a common prayer. I
think, for instance, that crowds have a prayer. When a crowd is
living together for a time, they come into the world again. A new
unity, like a nation or a parish, enters the world under the yoke of
love. This unity then casts its prayer in the direction of God.

Other times, a structure splits as an atom of language splits when
dialects are made out of it. Through the dialect language a harder,
more honest, or more closely-related prayer or number of prayers is
heard than the prayer of the basic language. The part of the basic
language which is closer to the new prayer splits off from the trap-

pings of the basic language and prays as a dialect, for it is yoked by a
new unity of love which has come into the world. In this way, the
dialects are a model of honesty for they refuse to live in the loose
atmosphere of the basic language and instead hold fast to an atmo-
sphere which is most native, dense, and honest.

But the person who is damned, what happened to him? I think
that he denied the truth. He refused to bow to the forms of truth and
instead continued to compose his own artificial forms as an anti-
Creator. And so, like a badger, he remained inside of himself for
eternity. The sermon *Ar an bPeaca Marfach* in *Seanmóirí Muighe
Nuadhat* states: 'Sinners usually like that which will never happen,
and dislike that which will be there forever.'[17] In this case, the
person never went visiting among the temples:

> It's the badger's habit to burrow down
> night and day in the dark.
> For the world from Earth to Heaven
> he wouldn't come to greet you.[18]
>   (Séamus Mac Cuarta)[19]

In the end he created a post-judgement body instead of the body
which God reserved for him. On the Day of Judgement, he will be
like a person with a ticket for dinner in his hand, and the name of
another person written on the ticket. He won't be let in because he
wasn't invited. One can say that he created a stranger, a person
outside of God's destiny—a person who was not invited. Or one can
say that he did not create or mould anything at all and that he will
enter eternity with a structure which is incarnated in a lie or in an
illusion or in a curse and that he must suffer this pretense forever.
Now he is nothing but a lie and he will be sent to hell, a place where
there isn't a single example of the sculpturing of truth, a place
which he and others like him created from their own disobedient
imagination. A false place. I have tried to explain the damned mind
in the following piece entitled 'Saoirse.' And I have to admit that I

felt this damned abstract freedom pressing on me while I was writing this preface.

I have to summarize the terms which I have used this far. The soul is called the structure. The action which comes out of the structure is a prayer. And the temple is the weak body or the weak state: for instance, in the case of a person it is his clay body, and in the case of architecture it is all the knowledge of architecture which is not startled.

It's also important that we answer the foregoing questions. What is the basic joyous image, the bedrock of which I was speaking? It is the hard, pure, elegant prayer of the thing which we contemplate— a part of the sculpturing of truth beyond ourselves. A pre-tasting of the pure form which will be surrounding us in eternity as one of the bodies of eternity. And how do we all recognize it? Because it startles us as the apostles were startled in the village of Emmaus: 'Was not our heart burning within us, whilst he spoke in this way, and opened to us the scriptures?'[20] Although it is outside of us, we touch the bedrock through our own prayer. And how is it possible to recognize the form of our own prayer if we do not rub it against something else? How else but in relation to, and in contact with, a true thing which is beyond ourselves and under the protection of truth? This is not unlike T. S. Eliot's idea of the 'objective co-relative.'[21]

But how do I know that the prayer of the thing outside of us constitutes the bedrock?

I said that a particular death startles us sooner than death as an abstract concept. Death in the abstract is a temple. A specific death is a prayer, one of the prayers of that temple. When a specific death occurs, death is active, it is saying its prayer. Death is startled at that time, and it living-startles us (if it does not kill us, and even then it could startle us into prayer). When we hear an account of a particular death and are startled because of it, it's in this way that that particular death comes easily to us in the form of a prayer. We feel it pressing against us as we feel the pulse of a current. We feel the basic image, the pressing bedrock, and we are startled. And because we are startled, if we wish to compose a poem, it is possible to do so at once. And it is easily done.[22] It is almost as easy to put this form into words as it would be to put a vest on a child. In this case, the words are always there, and they are marked by precise tailoring.

But if we make a reasonable attempt to write a poem on death, it is like going into a cold temple even though we ourselves are cold temples. For a long time, we are sterile, imperceptive, and lonely.

> Time passes wearily in Elphin tonight:
> last night I thought it passed wearily too;
> and though wearily I find today go by,
> yesterday lacked nothing in its weary length.[23]

We are digging and reading and coughing until we meet the bedrock—the Braille, the lung, the prayer. Then a start! This is the truth! This is the end of the journey! This is the marrow. This is the shoulder of God! We are released at once from the confinement of our own mind—from Elphin—from the storm of sterility—from hell. We are now outside of our own mind or above it like a robin.[24] What a great relief to hear that there is an outside, because until the start comes, we do not know that we are not inside. We don't know that the whole of life isn't lived inside. We do not know that anything else is there except ourselves. We stretched our minds out in the darkness of night and thank God there was something besides darkness there. A thing is beautiful. We are now traveling calmly through the length and breadth of truth. We have a support—a strong, sure support. There is an inexplicable precision in our voice. When we have written the poem, the lines become immutably set, as if they were a part of the existence beyond ourselves and as if someone else had written them. It was only that we saved them. It was us that came within range of the start. That was all.

As opposed to writing a poem on a particular event this is a long and tiring course, but in a way, it's more wonderful. Here we stir death without killing anyone. We only had the subject of death and we made death from it. But you have to admit that this time the vest does not fit the child as quickly, for the child is feeble and abstract because he came out of an incubator. But I believe that this child becomes agile after being incarnated in words so that after a while it isn't possible to distinguish him from a specific event. I believe that a poem ripens by itself after it has been stored for a while.

It seems to me that the prayer of the thing outside of us constitutes the bedrock for these reasons:

(a) We were always startled by something beyond ourselves (an event or subject of contemplation).
(b) We were startled quickly when this thing was active.
(c) And we had to search for the start when it was weak.

Now to judge the poem in terms of prayer. Let's say that the child is a working poet and that he composed a poem. What happened? He became lonely when he saw the horse. He empathized with horseness. He arrived in the darkness at the prayer or bedrock of horseness. The word-clothes came from the tailor, that is, from the predecessors of the child. It's clear now that the prayer of the horse went inside the clothes, that is, into the poem. An excitement is now felt under the clothes, a rhythm like trotting. But where did the prayer of the child go? Into the poem. But how? Isn't the poem trotting instead of crawling? But look more closely at the poem. This poem is a little world in itself about which no knowledge outside of itself can be found.

> 'How do you know, you who were trained in this land of the poem, that it is trotting?'
> 'Because it isn't crawling.'
> 'Is there any crawling at all in this poem?'
> 'No.'
> 'And how do you know what crawling is?'
> 'In relation to trotting.'

'But how in relation to trotting?'

'Because that is the kind of trotting it is—trotting which is not crawling.'

It's clear from this dialogue that the prayer of the child is found in the poem in proportion to the prayer of the horse.

I would like to name the specific things that I see in poetry:

(a) an open mind of a child
(b) solitude
(c) empathy
(d) a precision of form
(e) an affinity between prayer-forms: the start comes from this affinity, and it is the whole of poetry and of prayer. It is this affinity which causes the rhythm.
(f) a good team of tailors, i.e., the predecessors and the whole tradition of the poet.

In this country, there are people who say that the Irish language writers of our generation aren't traditional. I believe that they are mistaken. These people are looking at the writers from the yard. The writers are inside the language and not outside in the yard. They are praying in the temple of Irish and if they stir any prayer it must be the prayer of Irish. It's not possible to bend the language away from its source. It's not possible for any other prayer to come out of the temple of Irish but its own prayer. And I believe that it won't be long until this temple is transmitting its prayer with all of its force. At present, the writers are praying in the language for they need to wake up the language so that she will become active and start praying by her own will. And where will she go to pray but in the temples of the people? The writers will wake up the language and the awakened language will stir the people to speak in Irish.

I ask my readers to forgive the insignificance and sparseness of my own work.

NOTES

Editor's preface

1. 'Síorthaisteal ó mhise go mise'/'forever travelling from me to me [or self to self].' Ó Ríordáin, quoted in Seán Ó Coileáin, *Seán Ó Ríordáin: Beatha agus Saothar* (Dublin: An Clóchomhar, 1982, 1985), pp. 155–6.

2. Ó Ríordáin's work has appeared, for example, in Wes Davis (ed.), *An Anthology of Modern Irish Poetry* (Cambridge & London: Harvard University Press, 2010) and in Patrick Crotty (ed.), *Modern Irish Poetry: An Anthology* (Belfast: Blackstaff, 1995). However, the same few poems appear repeatedly and seem to emphasize a limited number of subjects. While these points to central themes in Ó Ríordáin's oeuvre, they are not the only ones and need to be seen in their wider context.

3. For example, Michael Davitt, 'Faobhar na Faille Siar in Anglia Sheán Uí Ríordáin,' in *Fís agus Teanga*, ed. by P. Reaney and M. Ó Conghaile (Indreabhán: Cló Iar-Chonnacht, 1999), p. 34; and Frank Sewell, 'For Seán Ó Ríordáin,' in *The New North: Contemporary Poetry from Northern Ireland*, ed. by Chris Agee (Winston-Salem, NC: Wake Forest Press, 2008, 2011), pp. 211–22.

4. John Montague, 'The Two Seáns,' *Smashing the Piano* (Oldcastle: Gallery Press, 1999), p. 58.

5. Seamus Heaney, 'Forked Tongues, Céilís and Incubators,' in *Fortnight*, No. 197 (Sept. 1983), 113–16.

6. Just as Daniel Corkery and James Joyce became, respectively for Ó Ríordáin (*ES* 51; *TÉB* 21), he in turn has become something of a 'second conscience' for current Irish-language poets such as Gearóid Mac Lochlainn.

7. Including *Tar Éis a Bháis: Aistí ar Sheán Ó Ríordáin*, ed. by Máiréad Ní Loingsigh (Indreabhán: Cló Iar-Chonnacht, 2008).

8. Ciaran Carson writes that he has been 'trying to translate [Ó Ríordáin's 'Malairt'] for about half of my life.' See Carson, '1940–49,' in T. Dorgan and N.

Duffy (eds), *Watching the River Flow: A Century in Irish Poetry* (Dublin: Poetry Ireland, 1999), p. 86.

9. Ó Coileáin, p. 209.

10. Ó Coileáin, p. 72.

11. Ó Coileáin, p. 209.

12. See Ó Ríordáin's poem 'Na Blascaodaí'/'The Blaskets.'

13. Translations of his work have already appeared in Japanese and French, for example.

14. Eavan Boland writing of the 'Irish poetry scene' in the 1950s and 1960s, seemingly unaware of Mhac an tSaoi's very significant contribution, i.e. her first and strongest collection, *Margadh na Saoire* (Dublin: Sáirséal & Dill, 1956).

15. See Ó Searcaigh, 'An lilí bhándearg'/'The pink lily,' in *Out in the Open* (Indreabhán: Cló Iar-Chonnacht, 1997), p. 236; Davitt, 'Ragham amú,' in *Sláinte*, ed. by M. Ó Conghaile (Indreabhán: Cló Iar-Chonnacht, 1995), p. 78. Note: *INNTI* was an influential literary (mainly poetry) journal and movement founded in 1970 by Michael Davitt. Leading members and contributors also included Liam Ó Muirthile, Gabriel Rosenstock and Nuala Ní Dhomhnaill.

16. Alan Titley, 'An Teanga Eile Leath-Leis,' in Ní Loingsigh (ed.), *Tar Éis a Bháis: Aistí ar Sheán Ó Ríordáin*, pp. 62–79 (pp. 76–7).

17. Ní Dhomhnaill, email correspondence, 4 March 2010; Mac Lochlainn, email correspondence, 13 October 2010.

18. Poet Padraic Fiacc's inclusive phrase.

19. Ó Ríordáin, quoted in the Irish-language anthology *Cnuasach 1966: Nuafhilíocht agus Gearrscéalta Nua*, ed. by Breandán S. Mac Aodha (Dublin: Scepter, 1966), p. 79.

20. Ó Ríordáin, quoted in Ó Coileáin, p. 4.

21. Notably, Ó Ríordáin's reading list is mostly comprised of male authors, but not exclusively so: he was deeply attached to Eibhlín Dhubh Ní Chonaill's 'Lament for Art O'Leary'; he was among the first to recognise the talent of Nuala Ní Dhomhnaill; and, despite passing arguments over purity of diction, he repeatedly acknowledged Máire Mhac an tSaoi's claim to the title of 'poet.' In his own work, moreover, there are clear echoes, for example, of Emily Dickinson in poems such as 'An Bás'/'Death.'

22. The doodles and drawings scattered throughout Ó Ríordáin's notebooks are almost exclusively of people's heads, reflecting his focus on the mind and personality of individuals, suggesting some distance (or even distaste) on his part regarding the body.

23. 'Is fadó a bhíos slogtha mura mbeadh mionscagadh so na dialainne'/'I would have been sunk long ago if it wasn't for this diary's fine-filtering [sifting].' Quoted in Ó Coileáin, p. 3.

24. See Titley, 'An Teanga Eile Leath-Leis,' pp. 76–7.

25. Quoted in Ó Coileáin, p. 212.

26. See Emerson, 'Self-reliance' in *Ralph Waldo Emerson: Essays and Poems*, ed. by T. Tanner (London: J. M. Dent Ltd./Everyman Library, 1992), pp. 23–46 (p. 30).

27. Seamus Heaney, 'Station Island XII,' in Heaney, *New Selected Poems 1966–1987* (London: Faber and Faber, 1990), p. 193.

28. Patrick Kavanagh, 'Self-Portrait,' in *Collected Pruse* [sic], second edition (London: Martin Brian and O'Keefe, 1973).

29. For Ó Ríordáin's own wry comment on this, see Ó Coileáin, pp. 211–12.

30. Quotes from 'Oilithreacht fám anam'/'Pilgrimage of my soul' and 'Cnoc Mellerí'/'Mount Melleray,' respectively.

31. See Ó Ríordáin, quoted in Ó Coileáin, p. 243; and V. Shklovsky, 'Art as Technique,' in *Debating Texts: a Reader in Twentieth-Century Literary Theory and Method*, third edition (Milton Keynes: Open University Press, 1987, 1990), pp. 48–56 (pp. 48–9).

32. W. E. Coles, *The Plural I* (New York: Holt, 1978).

33. Yeats, 'The Choice,' *W. B. Yeats: Collected Poems*, ed. by Augustine Martin (London: Vintage, 1990, 1992), p. 254.

34. Kavanagh, *Collected Poems* (London: MacGibbon and Kee, 1964), p. 19.

35. Translated in this collection by Mary O'Donoghue as 'she-poet.'

36. Ó Ríordáin, diary entry, 14 June 1961, quoted in Ó Coileáin, p. 203.

37. Ó Ríordáin, 'Máire Mhac an tSaoi,' *Irish Times*, 13 November 1975, quoted in Ó Coileáin, p. 369.

38. The poem appeared in print in his posthumous collection, *Tar Éis mo Bháis* (1978).

39. See Ó Coileáin, pp. 155–6.

40. See 'Cúl an tí'/'The back of the house.'

41. Quoted in Sewell, *Modern Irish Poetry: A New Alhambra* (Oxford: Oxford University Press, 2000), p. 27.

42. Eoghan Ó hAnluain, 'The Twentieth Century: Prose and Verse,' additional chapter in Aodh de Blacam, *Gaelic Literature Surveyed*, second edition (Dublin: Talbot Press, 1929, 1973), p. 391.

43. Ó Ríordáin, quoted in Ó Coileáin, pp. 2–3.

44. See the final poem in this selection. Please note that the poems included here from Ó Ríordáin's fourth, and posthumous, collection *Tar Éis mo Bháis* have been re-arranged (as far as possible) into an estimated chronological order.

45. Quote attributed to Joyce in Arthur Power, *From the Old Waterford House* (Waterford: Carthage Press, 1940), pp. 65–6.

46. Patrick Kavanagh, 'The Parish and the Universe,' in P. Kavanagh, *Collected Pruse* [sic] (London: Macgibbon and Kee, 1967), p. 282.

47. Ó Ríordáin, quoted in *Rogha an Fhile/The Poet's Choice*, ed. by Eoghan Ó Tuairisc (Dublin: Goldsmith Press, 1974), pp. 57–8.

48. Louis MacNeice, 'Snow,' *Collected Poems* (London: Faber and Faber, 1979, repr. 1986), p. 30.

49. See Ó Ríordáin, 'Oileán agus oileán eile'/'This island and the other island'; and 'Clónna über alles'/'Clones *über alles?*'

50. Ó Ríordáin, quoted in Ó Coileáin, pp. 155–6.

Afterword

1. This translation is based on the version in the first edition of *Eireaball Spideoige* published in 1952. A second edition was published in 1986 in which there are slight edits, the majority of which are minor changes in spelling and grammar due to standardization. Some of the more significant changes between the editions are included in these footnotes. For the translation, my aim is to stay as near as possible to the original Irish while keeping an ear for clarity and readability. In Irish, the prose has a thrilling strangeness and creativity which is held together by precise observations and utterly human moments of levity. To this end, a straightforward translation seems best suited. I want to thank Nuala Ní Dhomhnaill and Gráinne Ní Mhuirí for their help with the translation.

2. In the second edition, the father looks out and says, 'Sin capall Mháire ag dul thar bráid.' (That's Máire's horse going by.)

3. Terms such as 'múnla' (structure) or 'foirm' (form) are difficult to define outside of Ó Ríordáin's philosophical system. For these terms I consistently use one or two English equivalents so that the cogs and pins stay in place.

4. This sentence is omitted in the second edition.

5. Genesis 1: 12. 'And the earth brought forth the green herb, and such as yieldeth seed according to its kind, and the tree that beareth fruit, having seed each one according to its kind. And God saw that it was good.' (Douay-Rheims Version)

6. J. Maritain, *Oeuvres Complètes: Oeuvres de Jacques et Raïssa Maritain* (Fribourg: Éd Universitaires, 1994), vol. 14, 644–5; R. Maritain & J. Kernan, trans., *We have been Friends Together* (New York: Longman, 1943), 19–20.

7. L. Ó Rinn, *Mo Chara Stiofán* (Baile Átha Cliath: Oifig an tSoláthair, 1939), 85. Stephen MacKenna (1872–1935) was a journalist and translator, best known for his translation of Plotinus. (Dictionary of Irish Biography)

8. T. S. Eliot, *Collected Poems 1909–1935* (New York: Harcourt-Brace, 1936).

9. 'Dromchla' usually means 'a surface' in the sense of a 'crest' or 'ridge,' for example, 'dromchla na díleann'/the crest of the ocean (see Dinneen's dictionary). Here, however, the word 'dromchla' is combined with 'grinneall' meaning 'sea-bed', 'depths' or 'bottom.' Ó Ríordáin uses 'dromchla' throughout the preface as a term closer in meaning to 'deep surface' or 'foundation.'

10. See the poem 'An dall sa studio'/'The blind man in the studio.'

11. The word 'geit' means a 'fright,' 'start' or 'jump' (Dinneen). It is an important term in Ó Ríordáin's description of poetic creativity. I have translated it, depending on the use, sometimes as 'start' and, at other times, as 'startlement' or 'charge.'

12. The second edition clarifies: 'den XIIIú leabhar den *De Civitate Dei*' (of the thirteenth book of *De Civitate Dei*).

13. R. Bridges (ed.), *Poems of Gerard Manley Hopkins* (London: Humphrey Milford, 1918).

14. See the poem 'Siollabadh'/'Syllabication.'

15. In the second edition, the phrase 'mian na gcnoc síoraí' (the desire of the eternal hills) replaces 'mian na gcoillte síoraí' (the desire of the eternal woods) bringing the Irish closer in line with the bible passages that follow.

16. Genesis 49: 25–26. 'The God of thy father shall be thy helper, and the Almighty shall bless thee with the blessings of heaven above, with the blessings

of the deep that lieth beneath, with the blessings of the breasts and of the womb. The blessings of thy father are strengthened with the blessings of his fathers: until the desire of the everlasting hills should come; . . .' (DR).

17. *Seanmóirí Muighe Nuadhad* (The Maynooth Sermons) (Baile Átha Cliath: Muinntir Bhrúin agus Nualláin, 1906), Vol. 1, 157.

18. S. Ó Tuama (ed.) & T. Kinsella (trans.), *An Duanaire 1600–1900: Poems of the Dispossessed* (Dublin: Dolmen Press, 1981), 131.

19. Séamus 'Dall' Mac Cuarta (c. 1650–1732/3) was an important Ulster poet, who was blinded by an illness in his youth. (*Dictionary of Irish Biography*)

20. Luke 24:32. (DR)

21. T. S. Eliot (1888–1965) explains his understanding of the 'objective correlative' in his essay 'Hamlet and His Problems,' first published in *The Sacred Wood: Essays on Poetry and Criticism* (London: Methuen & Co., 1920).

22. This sentence is omitted in the second edition.

23. G. Murphy, trans., *Duanaire Finn* (London: Irish Texts Society, 1933), sec. 55, 195.

24. See the poem 'Adhlacadh mo mháthar'/My mother's burial.

NOTES ON THE TRANSLATORS

Denise Blake (née McGill) was born in Ohio and has lived in Letterkenny, Co. Donegal since 1969. Her poetry collections include *Take a Deep Breath* (2004) and *How to Spin Without Getting Dizzy* (2010). Alongside Seamus Heaney, she translated numerous poems in Cathal Ó Searcaigh's *Cois Tineadh i Mín a' Leá/By the Hearth in Mín a' Leá* (2005), a Poetry Book Society Recommended Translation.

Colm Breathnach was born and educated in Cork. He retired recently as a terminologist and translator for the Irish government. He has been published both by Coiscéim and Cló Iar-Chonnacht, and his collections include *Cantaic an Bhlabháin* (1991), *Scáthach* (1994), *An Fear Marbh* (1998), *Chiaroscuro* (2006) and *'Dánta' agus Dánta Eile* (2012).

Paddy Bushe writes in both English and Irish. His poetry collections, include *Poems with Amergin* (1989), *Teanga* (1990), *Digging Towards the Light* (1994), *In Ainneoin na gCloch* (2001), *Hopkins on Skellig Michael* (2001), *The Nitpicking of Cranes* (2004), and *To Ring in Silence: New and Selected Poems* (2008).

Ciaran Carson is a prolific poet, prose writer and translator. His poetry collections include *The Irish for No* (1987), *First Language* (1993), and *Collected Poems* (2008). He has translated *The Inferno of Dante Alighieri* (2002), *The Midnight Court* (2005) and *The Táin* (2007). He is also a musician, with music often woven into the subject matter and form of his work. He has written two texts on Irish traditional music, including *Last Night's Fun* (1996).

Celia de Fréine is a poet, playwright and screenwriter who writes in Irish and English. She has published five collections of poetry:

Faoi Chabáistí is Ríonacha (2001), *Fiacha Fola* (2004), *Scarecrows at Newtownards* (2005), *imram: odyssey* (2010), and *Aibítir Aoise: Alphabet of an Age* (2011).

Theo Dorgan is a poet, writer, lecturer and broadcaster whose works include *The Ordinary House of Love* (1991), *Rosa Mundi* (1995), *Sappho's Daughter* (1998), and *Greek* (2010). He has co-edited numerous texts, including *The Great Book of Ireland* (1991), *Revising the Rising* (1991), *Irish Poetry Since Kavanagh* (1996), *Watching the River Flow* (1999), and *The Great Book of Gaelic* (2002). He was Series Editor of publications by the European Poetry Translation Network.

Eilish Martin has two collections of poetry: *slitting the tongues of jackdaws* (1999) and *Ups Bounce Dash* (2008). Her work has been translated and anthologized in Mexico and Russia, for example, in *Word of Mouth: Slovo iz Ust* (St. Petersburg, 2004), and was included in *The White Page/An Bhileog Bhán: Twentieth Century Irish Women Poets* (1999).

Barry McCrea is professor of English and Comparative Literature and Keough Family College Chair of Irish Studies at the University of Notre Dame. He is the author of a novel, *The First Verse* (2005), and of the monograph *In the Company of Strangers: Family and Narrative in Dickens, Conan Doyle, Joyce, and Proust* (2011).

Noel Monahan has five collections of poetry all published by Salmon, Ireland: *Opposite Walls* (1991), *Snowfire* (1995), *Curse of The Birds* (2000), *The Funeral Game* (2004), and *Curve of the Moon* (2011). His poetry has been translated into Italian, Romanian, French and Russian.

Paul Muldoon's main collections of poetry are *New Weather* (1973), *Mules* (1977), *Why Brownlee Left* (1980), *Quoof* (1983), *Meeting The British* (1987), *Madoc: A Mystery* (1990), *The Annals of Chile* (1994), *Hay* (1998), *Poems 1968–1998* (2001), *Moy Sand and Gravel* (2002), *Horse Latitudes* (2006), and *Maggot* (2010). His translations include Nuala Ní Dhomhnaill's *The Astrakhan Cloak* (1993) and *The Fifty Minute Mermaid* (2007).

Mary O'Donoghue is a poet, fiction writer and translator. Her poetry collections include *Tulle* (2001) and *Among These Winters* (2007), and her work was anthologized in Bloodaxe's *The New Irish Poets* (2004). Her short stories have been widely published, and a debut novel, *Before the House Burns*, appeared in 2010. Together with Biddy Jenkinson and others, she co-translated the poems of Louis de Paor in his bilingual volume *agus rud eile de/and another thing* (2010).

Francis O'Hare is a poet and translator. His two main collections of poetry are *Falling into an O* (2007) and *Somewhere Else* (2011), which include translations from Spanish, French and Irish. Both were published by Lagan Press, Belfast, as was his collection of sonnets, *Alphaville: une étrange aventure de mon âme* (2009).

Mary O'Malley is a poet and teacher. Her poetry collections include *A Consideration of Silk* (1990), *Where the Rocks Float* (1993), *The Knife in the Wave* (1997) and *Asylum Road* (2001), all with Salmon Publishing; and *The Boning Hall*, featuring new and selected poems (2002) and *A Perfect V* (2006), both published by Carcanet.

Frank Sewell is a poet, translator and critic. His poems are anthologised, for example, in *The New North* (Wake Forest Press, 2008, 2011). His critical writing includes *Modern Irish Poetry* (2000); and among his translations are Cathal Ó Searcaigh's *Out in the Open* (1998), and (with Mitsuko Ohno) *On Two Shores: New & Selected Poems by Mutsuo Takahashi* (2006).

Peter Sirr is a poet, freelance writer and translator whose poetry collections include *Marginal Zones* (1984), *Talk, Talk* (1987), *Ways of Falling* (1991), *The Ledger of Fruitful Exchange* (1995), *Bring Everything* (2000), *Selected Poems* and *Nonetheless* (both 2004), and *The Thing Is* (2009), all published by Gallery Press.

Robert Welch (1947–2013), poet, novelist, critic and translator whose works include *A History of Verse Translation from the Irish* (1988), *Changing States: Transformations in Modern Irish Literature* (1993), *The Kilcolman Notebook* (a novel, 1994), *Secret Societies* (poems, 1997), *Tearmann* (a novel, 1997), *Forty Four* (translations of poems by Dana Podracka, 2005), *Constanza* (poems, 2010) and *Japhy Ryder ar Shleasaibh na Mangartan: Leabhar Beathaisnéise agus Critice* (2011).

ABOUT THE AUTHOR

Seán Ó Ríordáin (1916–1977) was born in County Cork and lived his life entirely in Ireland. He completed four poetry volumes, the last—*Tar Éis Mo Bháis*—published posthumously. He also wrote powerful, and often playful, opinion pieces for *The Irish Times* during his later years.